Summer

Recipes Inspired by Nature's Bounty

Time-Life Books is a division of Time Life Inc.
Time-Life is a trademark of Time Warner Inc. U.S.A.

TIME-LIFE CUSTOM PUBLISHING
Vice President and Publisher: Terry Newell
Associate Publisher: Teresa Hartnett
Managing Editor: Donia Ann Steele
Director of New Product Development: Quentin McAndrew
Director of Sales: Neil Levin
Director of Financial Operations: J. Brian Birky

WILLIAMS-SONOMA
Founder/Vice-Chairman: Chuck Williams
Book Buyer: Victoria Kalish

Produced by
WELDON OWEN INC.
President: John Owen
Vice President and Publisher: Wendely Harvey
Chief Financial Officer: Larry Partington
Associate Publisher: Lisa Chaney Atwood
Consulting Editor: Norman Kolpas
Copy Editor: Sharon Silva
Production Director: Stephanie Sherman
Production Manager: Jen Dalton
Production Editor: Katherine Withers Cobbs
Design: Angela Williams
Food Photographer: Penina
Food and Prop Stylist: Pouké
Assistant Food Photographer: Martin Dunham
Assistant Food Stylist: Michelle Syracuse
Illustrations: Thorina Rose
Co-Editions Director: Derek Barton

Production by Mandarin Offset, Hong Kong
Printed in China

First Printing 1997
10 9 8 7 6 5 4 3 2 1

Library of Congress
Cataloging-in-Publication Data:

Weir, Joanne
    Summer : recipes inspired by nature's bounty / Joanne Weir.
        p.   cm. -- (Williams-Sonoma seasonal celebration)
    Includes index.
    ISBN 0-7835-4607-6
    1. Cookery.   2. Summer.   I. Title.   II. Series.
TX714.W334 1997
641.5'64--DC20   96-35496
                                                  CIP

A Note on Weights and Measures:
All recipes include customary U.S. and metric measurements.
Metric conversions are based on a standard developed for these
books and have been rounded off. Actual weights may vary.

WILLIAMS-SONOMA SEASONAL CELEBRATION

Summer

Recipes Inspired by Nature's Bounty

Joanne Weir

Summer

Summer squashes are characterized by their thin, edible skins and seeds.

In summertime, nature bestows a bounty of diverse and flavorful ingredients. From farmers' markets to grocery stores to home gardens, the colorful wealth of the season is evident: bell peppers shading from green to richly burnished yellow to crimson, deep red vine-ripened tomatoes, slender green and purple beans, sunny yellow squashes.

Bushel baskets overflow with enticing tree fruits—cherries, peaches, nectarines, apricots, plums—that, at first bite, send juices coursing down the chin. Berries beckon with their jewellike colors. Honeydews, watermelons and cantaloupes conceal the promise of sweet refreshment. And everywhere the air is scented with fresh herbs, ready to enhance the taste and aroma of any food with which they are partnered.

These summer treasures may be transformed with only the simplest of culinary embellishments. Tomatoes join with peppers, onions, bread and olive oil to make gazpacho. Peppers marry with eggplant, fresh herbs and cheeses to fill a tempting calzone. Fresh basil, transformed into pesto, explodes with flavor. Summer fruits pack pies and tarts, flavor ice creams, and bubble up beneath a cobbler's golden topping. Such are summertime's elemental pleasures.

Selecting Summer Ingredients

Summer Vegetables. Many of the year's most flavorful vegetables ripen in summer, the most characteristic being vegetable fruits and soft-skinned summer squashes. When choosing **bell peppers (capsicums), chilies, tomatoes, cucumbers** or **eggplants (aubergines),** look for those that feel firm and have bright, glossy skins. The same applies to the many varieties of **summer squash,** with the added tip that you'll enjoy the best flavor and texture from smaller specimens. Perfectly ripe **avocados** yield to gentle finger pressure; still-hard ones will ripen at room temperature.

Look for **salad greens** that are crisp and bright, avoiding those with any signs of wilting or browning; smaller greens tend to be milder in flavor, a tip to keep in mind when buying the bitter varieties such as frisée. Crispness is also a sign of peak freshness for **snap beans**—green beans, purple beans, wax beans—which should cleanly break in half when bent. The best fresh **shell beans** come from pods barely plump and flexible, with no signs of softness; split open, the pods should feel moist within.

The finest **garlic** and **shallot** bulbs feel heavy and look firm, dry skinned and blemish free. Ginger should be free of moisture and wrinkles. **Potatoes** at their optimum feel heavy, look firm and are free of any sprouting eyes that betray prolonged storage.

Summer Fruits. Grown from earth soaked in springtime's showers, summer fruits brim with juice, and the best of each type will show clear signs of this blessing. Ready-to-eat **melons** are heavy for their size; ripe varieties of smaller melons yield slightly when pressed with a thumb and, if sniffed closely, give off a hint of their sweet, musky aroma. When choosing watermelons from a farmers' market or roadside stand, you may be fortunate enough to be indulged in the old-fashioned practice of being offered a plug of the melon to sample. If not, seek out firm, evenly colored and well-shaped specimens with rinds that are blemish free and appear waxy.

The best **berries** look plump with juice and have bright, deep, clear colors and sweet aromas. If they have been packed in containers, examine the bottoms for signs of juice leakage, an indication that crushed or moldy specimens might be buried within.

Tree **fruits** should feel heavy for their size. Ripe fruit yields slightly to finger pressure, but most firm fruits will ripen at home at room temperature. Inspect them for blemishes or bruises: even tough-looking figs have surprisingly fragile skins. Good plums also usually have a hint of harmless, hazy white bloom on their otherwise shiny skins. Mature peaches, nectarines and apricots carry a sweet perfume, offering just a hint of the rich flavor within.

Summer Seasonings. The scent of fresh-picked **herbs** are the summertime's kitchen perfume. Choose herbs with brightly hued leaves free of wilting, blemishes or discoloration. For the best selection, quality and freshness, grow them yourself; all those shown on pages 12–13 thrive on sunny windowsills, in window boxes, on patios or in gardens. Start them from seed or from plants from a nursery specializing in culinary herbs.

Use caution when seeking edible summer **flowers.** Those from florists are likely to have been chemically treated, rendering them potentially harmful. For safety's sake, buy flowers only from a source—be it a farmers' market stall or other specialty grower—that can attest to growing conditions free of pesticides or other potentially harmful additives. Better still, grow them yourself.

When the husks and silks are pulled back from fresh corn cobs, the kernels beneath should appear smooth and plump.

Bell peppers, like tomatoes, range in color from deep green to yellow to orange to crimson red.

Ripe summer peaches should feel tender to the touch and smell sweet.

Summer Vegetables

1. Bell Peppers

Bell-shaped peppers (capsicums) with crisp flesh and a flavor that becomes even sweeter as the summer sun ripens them to shades varying from yellow to orange to red. The flesh is at its most digestible when the pepper has been roasted and peeled. Roasted or raw, peppers should be stemmed, ribbed and seeded before use (see summer techniques, page 14).

2. Poblano Chili Pepper

Variety of milder chili pepper with rich, relatively spicy flavor. Poblano chilies resemble tapered, triangular bell peppers and range in color from dark green to brick.

3. Pasilla Chili Pepper

Slightly elongated chili pepper characterized by its moderately hot taste with a hint of berry. Ranges in color from dark green to almost black. Also known as chilaca.

4. Jalapeño Chili Pepper

Common variety of spicy chili, measuring 2–3 inches (5–7.5 cm) in length and about 1 inch (2.5 cm) wide. Sold in its immature dark green and, less often, ripened red forms.

5. Serrano Chili Pepper

Smaller, more slender and significantly hotter than the jalapeño variety. Available in both its green and red forms.

6. Avocados

This favorite summer vegetable is grown in temperate climates worldwide, making it available almost year-round. Of the several varieties available, the Hass (sometimes spelled Haas) pictured here is preferred for it rich flavor and especially smooth texture. It may be recognized by its dark green, pebbly textured skin, which turns almost black when the avocado is ripe. A second popular variety, the Fuerte, has smooth, dark green skin.

7. Tomatoes

Vine-ripened tomatoes define summer for many people. Many different varieties may be grown at home or found in farmers' markets or well-stocked produce shops, including widely available spherical beefsteak tomatoes and elongated plum tomatoes, also known as Romas; popular, descriptively named little cherry tomatoes (far right), in both red and yellow; medium-sized, spherical orange or yellow tomatoes; and tiny, orange or yellow pear- or teardrop-shaped tomatoes. Also seek out rarer heirloom tomato varieties, which come in varied patterns of white, red and yellow.

8. Cucumbers

Cool, crisp, refreshing vegetable at its peak in summer's heat, usually eaten raw or pickled. Most common varieties are little pickling cucumbers; plump, dark-green-skinned, nearly seedless English or hothouse cucumbers (pictured at right); and long, slender Mediterranean or Middle Eastern cucumbers. Also look for, or try growing, rarer varieties such as the mild, spherical, yellow-skinned lemon cucumber (also pictured).

9. Eggplants

Of Asian origin, the eggplant (aubergine) migrated across the Middle East to Europe, reaching Italy by the 15th century. Its multitude of varieties include among them an ivory-skinned type resembling a goose egg, the source of its English name. The two most common types of this high-summer vegetable are the large, plump globe eggplant (pictured near right) and the long, slender Asian eggplant (pictured far right). The latter has fewer seeds and is considered to have a finer flavor and texture.

10. Zucchini

Also known as courgettes, slender, cylindrical members of the squash family, with soft, dark

Onion Family

16. Shallots
Relative of the onion, with smaller bulbs thought by some to resemble in taste a cross between onion and garlic.

17. Garlic
Pungent bulb, harvested in early summer, whose individual cloves, whether whole, chopped, crushed or puréed, raw or cooked, season a wide variety of savory dishes.

Beans and Seeds

18. Cranberry Beans
Variety of fresh shell beans, available from midsummer through fall, whose white pods and beans are streaked with cranberry red.

19. Purple Beans
Variety of wax beans, eaten whole like green beans, with deep purple pods that turn green when cooked.

20. Wax Beans
Also called yellow beans, these fresh, edible pods are distinguished by their waxlike sheen.

21. Green Beans
Refers to any of several different varieties of fresh beans eaten whole. Blue Lakes (pictured at left) and Kentucky Wonders are among those with the best flavor and texture.

22. Haricots Verts
French term for tender green beans harvested when immature, with very slender pods measuring no more than about 3 inches (7.5 cm) in length.

23. Corn
Native to Central America, corn begins to arrive in early summer and continues into early autumn. Yellow and white varieties are commonly available, with the former generally carrying a more intense corn flavor and the latter a sweeter taste. Look for yellow-white hybrids at farmers' markets and specialty stores.

Roots and Tubers

24. Yukon Gold Potatoes
Medium-sized waxy-fleshed potatoes prized for their golden color and rich, buttery flavor. A similar variety is the Yellow Finn. Both are ideal for baking, panfrying, mashing and gratins.

25. Ginger
Pungent, sweet-hot seasoning of Asian origin. Although it resembles a root, it is in fact the underground stem, or rhizome, of the tropical ginger plant. Available year-round, it is at its peak in summer.

green skin and tender, pale green flesh. Smaller specimens have a finer flavor and texture and tiny edible seeds. Also available in other varieties, including yellow zucchini and striped or spherical Italian types.

11. Pattypan Squashes
Small, mild summer squash with pale green skin and a shape resembling a flattened, scallop-edged top. Also known as custard or cymling squash. Slightly larger and plumper varieties include the green or yellow scallopini squash.

12. Yellow Crookneck Squashes
Similar in size to zucchini, a golden-skinned summer squash with pale yellow flesh, a rounded base and a swanlike, slender neck.

13. Zucchini Flowers
Delicate blossoms of the vegetable, sold separately or sometimes still attached to baby zucchini in farmers' and specialty produce markets. Best used on the day of purchase.

Leafy Vegetables

14. Red Leaf Lettuce
Mild lettuce with long, medium-green leaves fringed in reddish brown.

15. Frisée
Head of frilly leaves with a bitter edge of flavor at its mildest in the paler inner leaves. At its best in early summer.

Summer Fruits

Melons

1. Honeydew Melons

Although the most common honeydew melon has a pale yellow, waxy rind and pale green flesh, other types in a range of colors are now available. Orange honeydew has a flavor similar to cantaloupe, while the bright yellow honeydew has milky-colored flesh and a tropical, almost-pineapplelike taste. The green-and-orange Temptation variety combines the flavor of honeydew with a hint of cantaloupe. All have juicy, tender flesh—hence the dew part of their name. Most are also notable for their strong perfume that some people liken to honey. Available from early summer into early autumn.

2. Persian Melons

Resembling oversized cantaloupes with deep green or golden rinds covered in a tan weblike pattern, these melons have moist, fragrant, orange or salmon flesh and a mild, not overly sweet flavor similar to that of the cantaloupe. In season from early summer to early autumn. The name pays tribute to the melon's Middle Eastern origins.

3. Cantaloupes

One of the oldest varieties of melon, named after the town of Cantalupa, Italy. Their familiar tan netlike rinds conceal firm, moist orange flesh with a fairly firm texture and a sweet and fragrant, slightly musky flavor. At their peak throughout the summer.

4. Watermelons

Among the oldest known melons, distinguished by their large size and hard, deep green, mottled green or green-and-white rinds. Many varieties exist. Whether the flesh is rosy red, deep pink or bright yellow, and whether it has the familiar shiny dark brown or black seeds or is seedless, all share a characteristic crisp, slightly granular consistency coupled with the refreshingly high water content and appealing sweetness for which the melon is prized.

5. Casaba Melons

Available from late summer to early autumn, these melons are distinguished by their deeply wrinkled, yellow to pale green rinds and moderately large spherical shape tapering to a point at the stem end. Prized for their pale green, highly sweet, juicy flesh reminiscent of honeydew.

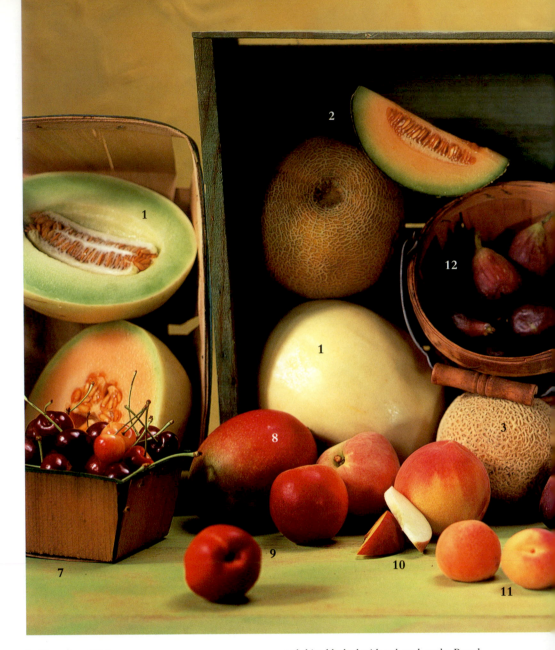

6. Crenshaw Melons

Teardrop-shaped melons with thin, smooth yellow-orange rinds. Their flesh, ranging from orange to salmon-pink, is highly aromatic, juicy and sweet, with a notable hint of spice. Harvested from mid- to late summer. Sometimes called Cranshaw melons.

Tree Fruits

7. Cherries

Sweet, juicy cherries enjoy a brief season in markets, harvested from the end of spring through midsummer. Most common are the ruby-red to almost purple-black Bing (pictured above) and Lambert varieties, followed by scarcer, more delicately flavored cherries with yellow flesh and skins blushed with red, such as the Royal Ann (also pictured) and Rainier varieties.

8. Mangoes

Crops from Florida, Mexico and the Caribbean, which begin producing in spring, continue to yield this tropical fruit, a native of India, into high summer. Soft and juicy as a peach, the yellow-orange flesh has a sweet, highly aromatic flavor. Harvested when still green, mangoes ripen easily at home when stored at room temperature; once ripe, they may be refrigerated for up to a week. To prepare a mango, score the slightly leathery skin lengthwise into quarters and peel it off, then cut off the flesh in two thick slices from either side of the large, flat pit. Trim the remaining fruit from around the pit's edges.

Several varieties may be found in markets year-round, but summer sees an abundance of such types as the purple-black Black Mission fig (pictured in bucket), whose soft skin conceals intensely flavored, sweet pink flesh; the Calimyrna (pictured below center), a California hybrid of the Turkish Smyrna fig with green skin, white to pale pink flesh, and a sweet, nutlike taste; and the Kadota, a small, yellowish green fig with sweet purple-pink flesh.

13. Plums

Plums are among the most ancient of tree fruits. More than 2,000 different hybrids are grown throughout the world, many of them developed within the past two centuries. Depending upon variety, they arrive in markets anywhere from late spring to the earliest days of autumn. Early summer plums, shown here, include the red-skinned Red Beauty and the purple-tinged Santa Rosa (in basket), and the blackish red Black Beauty (below left).

Berries

14. Blackberries

Available from the first days of summer almost to season's end, these glossy, plump, purple-black berries (pictured here in their unripened form), which still grow wild in some areas, are enjoyed for their rich, almost winelike flavor and juiciness.

15. Raspberries

Plump berries enjoyed for their juiciness and their delicate, sweet flavor with just a hint of tartness. Most familiar are red raspberries, although pale gold, purple and almost-black varieties also exist. All are highly perishable and should be eaten within 2 days of purchase. Grown in cooler climates and available throughout the summer, raspberries will be at their peak approaching midseason.

16. Blueberries

At their best from June through midsummer, these small, round, smooth-skinned berries abound in rich-tasting, sweet and flavorful juice. Rare wild blueberries are generally smaller in size and have a more intense flavor than the cultivated variety.

17. Boysenberries

This stout, deep purple hybrid of the blackberry, red raspberry and loganberry was developed by Rudolph Boysen and popularized by Walter and Cordelia Knott, founders of the Knott's Berry Farm amusement park in Southern California. Grown in lesser quantities than those other berries from which they are derived, boysenberries take some sleuthing in well-stocked groceries and farmers' markets.

9. Nectarines

Sometimes incorrectly referred to as a hybrid of the peach and the plum, nectarines are in fact a relative of the peach and are notable for their pleasantly smooth, fuzz-free skins and the sweet flesh whose juiciness inspired their name.

10. Peaches

Hundreds of different peach types exist, grouped variously as cling peaches, including such familiar types as Maycrest and Spring-crest, in which the fruits' pulp clings tightly to the pit; or freestone, including the Elberta and O'Henry varieties among others, from which the pit may be easily and neatly removed. Peaches also, depending upon variety, may

have yellow-orange flesh or paler yellow "white" flesh. All of them, and particularly those harvested later in summer, have the rich, almost melting juiciness and the deeply perfumed flavor for which the fruit is appreciated.

11. Apricots

Although they originated in China, where they were cultivated more than 4,000 years ago, apricots derive their name from the Latin for "precocious," an indication that these fruits, which resemble small, yellow to deep orange peaches, arrive in markets on the threshold of summer.

12. Figs

Often mentioned in the Bible, these small, pear-shaped fruits thrive worldwide in semidesert areas.

Summer Seasonings

Herbs

1. Thyme

An ancient herb of the eastern Mediterranean, with fragrant, clean-tasting small leaves that, whether fresh or dried, complement poultry, light meats, seafood or vegetables. Lemon thyme, which has a zesty citrus flavor, should be used with discretion, although it goes particularly well with seafood, poultry and even some fruit desserts.

2. Marjoram

A close relative of oregano, but with a milder, yet still pungent flavor and heady aroma that is well suited to seasoning seafood, poultry, meats, egg dishes and vegetable fruits such as eggplant (aubergine) and tomatoes. Use in fresh form, if possible, to show off its delicate flavor.

3. Sage

Strongly flavored, highly aromatic herb, used either fresh or dried, and generally with some discretion. Popular in the cuisines of Europe and the Middle East, it goes particularly well with fresh or cured pork, lamb, veal or poultry, and also appears in sauces and salads.

4. Rosemary

Mediterranean herb, used either fresh or dried. The needlelike leaves, sometimes decked in tiny blue flowers, have a highly aromatic flavor well suited to lamb, veal, pork, poultry, seafood and vegetables. Use sparingly, as the strong taste can overpower dishes. Summertime grilling, however, allows more extravagant additions of the herb; its woody branches can be thrown on hot coals to produce a fragrant smoke or stripped of their leaves and used as skewers that impart subtle flavor.

5. Chives

Slender shoots of a plant related to the onion, used fresh to impart a mild, almost sweet onion flavor. Although chives are available dried in the seasonings section of food stores, fresh chives possess the best flavor.

6. Oregano

A hardy perennial form of marjoram, also sometimes known as wild marjoram. It has a more powerful, pungent flavor than its milder fresh cousin, especially when dried.

Goes well with a wide range of savory dishes, particularly those featuring tomatoes and other vegetables.

7. Basil

A spicy-sweet herb popular in Italian and French kitchens. Grows abundantly in summer and shares a special affinity with the season's vine-ripened tomatoes, whether eaten raw in salads or cooked in sauces. Also good with other vegetables, seafood, chicken and rice dishes.

8. Parsley

Popular fresh herb that originated in southern Europe and is still widely used there and in other Western cuisines to season and garnish a wide range of savory dishes. Available in two main types: the more common curly-leaf parsley, a popular garnish, and flat-leaf parsley, also known as Italian parsley, which has a more pronounced flavor and is preferred for use as a seasoning.

9. Mint

Fragrant herb with a sprightly, cooling flavor that is especially welcome in both savory and sweet warm-weather dishes ranging from lamb, poultry and vegetables to fruit and chocolate desserts. Mint grows so well in gardens that, unchecked, it can overrun other plants. Spearmint, the most common variety, has a strong

13. Purple Basil
Several varieties of the popular summer herb have reddish purple leaves, including dark opal basil and purple ruffle basil. Their flavors tend to be stronger and spicier than ordinary green basil, calling for more judicious use; the leaves also make a particularly attractive garnish.

14. Cilantro
Botanically related to the carrot, this green, leafy herb resembles flat-leaf (Italian) parsley, but has a sharp, aromatic, notably astringent flavor. Used for seasoning a wide range of savory dishes in the kitchens of Latin America, the Middle East and Asia. Also commonly referred to as fresh coriander or Chinese parsley.

Flowers and Spices

15. Nasturtiums
Members of the watercress family, these yellow to bright orange to orange-red blossoms have a distinctive peppery taste recalling that leafy vegetable. Green nasturtium leaves may also be eaten.

16. Pansies
Delicate flowers that contribute a subtle perfume and colors ranging from orange to deep violet.

17. Roses
The petals of this familiar flower lend their delicate perfume and wide rainbow of vibrant colors as both fresh and crystallized garnishes.

18. Borage
Bright purple, small, star-shaped blossoms of an herb with a mild cucumber flavor that grows wild throughout the Mediterranean and in similar climates.

19. Lavender
Sweetly fragrant purple flowers of a plant related to mint, adding bright color and heavy perfume to savory and sweet dishes. Dried lavender has a much more intense flavor than the fresh blossoms.

20. Vanilla Beans
These dried aromatic pods of an orchid variety native to southern Mexico are one of the world's most popular sweet flavorings. Vanilla beans from Madagascar are generally considered best. To remove the tiny, flavorful seeds from a vanilla bean, split the bean in half lengthwise with a small, sharp knife. Then use the tip of the knife to scrape out the seeds within each half. The scraped-out pods may be buried in a jar filled with granulated sugar to make vanilla sugar.

flavor and is generally preferred for seasoning. Try milder peppermint as well, or such distinctively scented varieties as apple mint and orange mint.

10. Summer Savory
This green herb has a slightly peppery taste that highlights the flavors of beans, tomatoes, seafood and poultry.

11. Bay Leaves
Pungent, spicy dried whole leaves of the bay laurel tree, which grows abundantly in the Mediterranean and in similar sunny climates such as that of California. Commonly used as a seasoning in simmered dishes, including soups and braises or stews of meat, poultry or seafood; in marinades for those same main ingredients; and in pickling mixtures. French bay leaves, sometimes found in specialty-food shops, possess a milder, sweeter flavor than those from California.

12. Dill
The fine, feathery fresh leaves thrive in full summer sunlight and yield a sweet, aromatic flavor that wonderfully complements pickling brines, vegetables, seafood (especially salmon), chicken, veal and pork.

Summer Techniques

THE SIMPLE TECHNIQUES demonstrated here typify the ease with which summer produce is prepared. In each, the goal is to highlight the natural flavors and textures of vegetables that have ripened in the warm, bright sunshine. Tomatoes are freed of their peels and seeds. Peppers—both mild bells and spicy fresh chilies—are seeded and then are often quickly roasted under the broiler to remove their skins and intensify their taste. Fresh herbs are chopped or shredded, the better to blend their aromatic flavors with those of other ingredients.

What comes next is often the simplest presentation—tossing tomatoes with cucumbers, bread and dressing to make a rustic salad, for example, or letting the warmth of a risotto coax the heady perfume from a garnish of basil chiffonade. Summer's culinary pleasures, after all, are meant to be enjoyed at leisure, in the sunshine or beneath balmy evening skies.

Seeding & Deribbing Bell Peppers

Before bell peppers (capsicums) are used, their flavorless, indigestible seeds and white ribs should be removed.

Using a sharp knife, cut the pepper in half through its stem end. With your fingers, pull out the stem and attached seed cluster. Pull out the white ribs and any remaining seeds.

Roasting & Peeling Bell Peppers

Roasting loosens the tough skins of peppers and partially cooks their flesh, making them tender and intensifying their natural sweetness.

Preheat a broiler (griller). Place prepared pepper halves, cut sides down, on a baking sheet. Roast until evenly blistered and blackened. Remove the peppers and drape with aluminum foil.

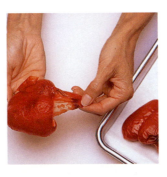

Leave the roasted peppers covered to steam and cool for about 10 minutes. Then, using your fingertips or, if necessary, a paring knife, peel away the blackened skins.

Peeling Tomatoes

Although summer salad recipes often call for nothing more than coring and slicing tomatoes, cooked or more refined raw dishes often require peeling off the vegetables' shiny skins before use.

Using a paring knife, cut out the core from the stem end of the tomato. At the opposite end, score an X in the skin. Bring a pot three-fourths full of water to a boil and fill a bowl with ice water.

Immerse the tomatoes in the boiling water for 15–20 seconds. Using a slotted spoon, transfer them to the ice water. When cool, peel away the skins, using the knife and starting at the X.

Seeding Tomatoes

Tomatoes contain watery pockets, or "sacs," of indigestible seeds that can dilute the consistency or mar the appearance of some dishes. The seeds are easily removed.

Cut the tomato in half crosswise. Hold each half over a bowl or the sink and squeeze gently to force out the seed sacs. Or use a fingertip or a small spoon to scoop them out.

Seeding Fresh Vegetables

Some summer vegetables, such as the cucumber and chili shown here, require specialized seeding techniques. Note that chilies contain oils that can burn. Wash your hands and do not touch your eyes after handling them.

To seed a cucumber, cut it in half lengthwise. Using a teaspoon, scoop out the seeds along the length of each half before cutting up the cucumber.

To seed a fresh chili, cut it in half through its stem end. Using the tip of the knife, cut out the stem, pale ribs and all attached seeds from each half; then scrape out any remaining seeds.

Cutting Fresh Herbs

Cutting fresh herbs helps to release their flavors before adding them to recipes. Basil, owing to the size and shape of its leaves, is easily shredded by a simple method.

Neatly stack about 6 good-sized fresh basil leaves and roll them tightly lengthwise to make a cigar shape. Using a paring knife, thinly slice the roll crosswise to make fine "chiffonade" threads.

Summer Basics

BASIL PESTO

Pesto comes from Liguria, in the northwestern corner of Italy. There, the basil is picked when less than 6 inches (15 cm) tall to ensure that the leaves are tender and sweet. If they are tough, thick or have been growing in the sun too long, the finished pesto may be bitter.

1   teaspoon olive oil

¼   cup (1¼ oz/37 g) pine nuts

1½   cups (1½ oz/45 g) packed fresh basil leaves, carefully rinsed and well dried

¼   cup (¼ oz/7 g) flat-leaf (Italian) parsley leaves, carefully rinsed and well dried

4   cloves garlic, minced

½   cup (4 fl oz/125 ml) extra-virgin olive oil

¾   cup (3 oz/90 g) freshly grated Parmesan cheese

     salt and freshly ground pepper

IN A FRYING PAN over medium heat, warm the olive oil. Add the pine nuts and cook, stirring constantly, until light golden brown, 3–4 minutes. Remove from the heat and let cool.

In a blender or a food processor fitted with the metal blade, combine the basil, parsley, pine nuts, garlic, extra-virgin olive oil and Parmesan. Process at high speed until well mixed, about 1 minute. Stop and scrape down the sides, then continue to process until smooth, about 1 minute longer, stopping to scrape down the sides as needed. Season to taste with salt and pepper. *Makes about 1¼ cups (10 fl oz/310 ml)*

BASIL-MINT PESTO

Follow the directions for basil pesto, substituting 1 cup (1 oz/ 30 g) packed fresh mint leaves for the parsley.

FRESH TOMATO SAUCE

Here is a good way to use all those misshapen or slightly bruised tomatoes you may have accumulated from your garden. Make batches of this sauce; frozen, it keeps well for up to 3 months.

5   lb (2.5 kg) tomatoes, cored and quartered

1   small red (Spanish) onion, peeled but left whole

3   fresh basil sprigs

4   cloves garlic

     salt and freshly ground pepper

IN A LARGE POT over medium-high heat, combine the tomatoes, onion, basil and garlic. Bring to a boil, reduce the heat to medium-low and simmer, uncovered, until much of the liquid has evaporated, about 2 hours.

Remove the onion and discard. Pass the sauce through a food mill fitted with the fine disk into a clean bowl. Alternatively, let cool slightly and purée the sauce in a food processor fitted with the metal blade, then strain through a coarse-mesh sieve into a clean bowl. Season to taste with salt and pepper. Serve immediately, or let cool completely, cover and refrigerate for up to 3 days or freeze for up to 3 months. *Makes about 3 cups (24 fl oz/750 ml)*

Barbecue Sauce

Use this sauce for chicken, ribs, beef or pork. If you have leftover barbecue sauce, combine it with an equal amount of mayonnaise and use it as a topping for hamburgers.

1	tablespoon vegetable oil
1	small yellow onion, minced
1	cup (8 fl oz/250 ml) tomato purée
3	tablespoons Dijon mustard
¼	cup (2 fl oz/60 ml) fresh lemon juice
¼	cup (2 oz/60 g) firmly packed brown sugar
2	tablespoons Worcestershire sauce
2	tablespoons hot-pepper sauce
¼	teaspoon ground allspice
¼	teaspoon ground ginger
¼	cup (2 fl oz/60 ml) water
	salt and ground pepper

IN A SAUCEPAN over medium heat, warm the oil. Add the onion and sauté until soft, about 10 minutes.

Add the tomato purée, mustard, lemon juice, brown sugar, Worcestershire sauce, hot-pepper sauce, allspice, ginger, water and salt and pepper to taste. Stir well. Bring to a boil, reduce the heat to low and simmer slowly, uncovered, until the sauce thickens, 5–10 minutes.

Remove from the heat and let cool. Use immediately, or cover and refrigerate for up to 4 days or freeze for up to 4 months. *Makes about 2 cups (16 fl oz/500 ml)*

Sparkling Fruit Wine

The best part of this sparkling summer cooler is the wine-marinated fruit at the bottom of each glass; be sure to offer spoons so guests can eat the fruit once they have drunk the wine.

½	bottle (1½ cups/12 fl oz/375 ml) Gewürztraminer, chilled
1	cup (8 fl oz/250 ml) peach nectar, chilled
1	lime, cut into 8 thin slices
1	peach or nectarine, halved, pitted and cut into small wedges
1	plum, halved, pitted and cut into small wedges
½	cup (2 oz/60 g) blackberries
½	bottle (1½ cups/12 fl oz/375 ml) Champagne or sparkling wine, chilled
	ice cubes

IN A LARGE PITCHER, stir together the Gewürztraminer and peach nectar. Reserve 6 lime slices for a garnish. Add the remaining lime slices, peach or nectarine wedges, plum wedges and blackberries to the pitcher. Chill for 1 hour.

Just before serving, stir in the Champagne or sparkling wine and ice cubes. Pour into wine glasses, distributing some of the fruit into each glass. Place a lime slice on the rim of each glass and serve well chilled. *Makes 4 cups (32 fl oz/1 l); serves 6*

Ginger-Peach Lemonade

A refreshing change of pace from typical summer lemonade, this minty drink can be spiked with a splash of rum for a summer cocktail. Look for ginger-peach tea bags in well-stocked markets or specialty-food stores.

5	cups (40 fl oz/1.25 l) water
2	ginger-peach tea bags
10	fresh mint leaves, plus mint sprigs for garnish
¼	cup (2 oz/60 g) sugar
¾	cup (6 fl oz/180 ml) fresh lemon juice
4	drops vanilla extract (essence)
1	tablespoon orange flower water
	ice cubes

IN A SAUCEPAN over high heat, bring 2 cups (16 fl oz/500 ml) of the water to a boil. Remove from the heat and add the tea bags, mint leaves and sugar. Stir to dissolve the sugar and let stand for 10 minutes.

Add the remaining 3 cups (24 fl oz/750 ml) water, the lemon juice, vanilla and orange flower water. Stir well, cover and chill for 1 hour.

Strain through a fine-mesh sieve into a pitcher. To serve, fill tall glasses with ice cubes, pour in the lemonade and garnish with mint sprigs. *Makes about 6 cups (48 fl oz/1.5 l); serves 6*

openers

Tomato and Onion Tart

3   ripe but firm tomatoes, 8–10 oz (250–315 g) total, cut into slices ¼ inch (6 mm) thick

1   cup (5 oz/155 g) all-purpose (plain) flour, frozen for 1 hour

⅓   cup (1½ oz/45 g) cake (soft-wheat) flour, frozen for 1 hour

¼   teaspoon salt

¾   cup (6 oz/185 g) unsalted butter, cut into pieces, frozen for 1 hour

2   teaspoons fresh lemon juice, chilled

¼   cup (2 fl oz/60 ml) ice water

1   cup (4 oz/125 g) shredded mozzarella cheese

½   cup (2 oz/60 g) freshly grated Parmesan cheese

1½   tablespoons chopped fresh oregano

¼   cup (1 oz/30 g) thinly sliced yellow onion, separated into rings

In France, simple country tarts like this one often form the centerpiece of a sunny picnic lunch. If you are short of time, ¾ pound (375 g) store-bought puff pastry can be substituted for the homemade.

PLACE THE TOMATO SLICES on paper towels and let drain for 1 hour.

Place both flours, the salt and butter in a food processor fitted with the metal blade and pulse until the mixture resembles pea-size crumbs. Transfer to a bowl. In a small cup, combine the lemon juice and ice water and add to the bowl. Using a fork, mix until the dough almost holds together.

Turn out the dough onto a lightly floured work surface and press together to form a rough rectangle shape. Large chunks of butter will be visible. Using a rolling pin, roll out into a rectangle about 8 by 12 inches (20 by 30 cm) and ½ inch (12 mm) thick. Fold in the 8-inch (20-cm) sides to meet in the center. Then fold in half to make a rough square forming 4 layers. This is your first turn.

Turn the dough a quarter of a turn and roll out again into a rectangle 8 by 12 inches (20 by 30 cm) and ½ inch (12 mm) thick. Repeat the folding. This is your second turn. Again make a quarter turn and roll out into the same-sized rectangle. Now fold into thirds as you would a business letter. Wrap in plastic wrap and chill for 1 hour.

Position a rack in the top part of an oven. Preheat to 400°F (200°C).

Roll out the dough on a lightly floured work surface into a round 12 inches (30 cm) in diameter. Trim the edges so that they are even, and then crimp to form sides ½ inch (12 mm) thick. Transfer to an ungreased baking sheet and sprinkle evenly with the mozzarella, ¼ cup (1 oz/30 g) of the Parmesan and the oregano. Arrange the tomato slices in concentric circles, overlapping slightly, on the cheese. Scatter the onion rings and then the remaining ¼ cup (1 oz/30 g) Parmesan over the tomatoes.

Bake until the crust is golden and the top is crispy, 25–35 minutes. Serve hot. *Makes one 10-inch (25-cm) tart; serves 6–8*

There is no fire without some smoke.

—John Heywood

Smoked Shellfish Quesadillas with Fresh Corn Salsa

For the salsa:

2   cups (12 oz/375 g) corn kernels (from 3 ears)

5   tablespoons (½ oz/15 g) chopped fresh cilantro (fresh coriander)

3   green (spring) onions, thinly sliced

3   tablespoons fresh lime juice

½–1 fresh jalapeño or serrano chili pepper, seeded and minced

     salt and freshly ground pepper

For the quesadillas:

6   oz (185 g) smoked shellfish such as mussels, shrimp (prawns) or scallops

5   green (spring) onions, thinly sliced

¾   cup (3 oz/90 g) shredded pepper Jack cheese

¾   cup (3 oz/90 g) shredded mozzarella cheese

¾   cup (3 oz/90 g) shredded white Cheddar cheese

6   flour tortillas, each 8–9 inches (20–23 cm) in diameter

These smoky quesadillas make an ideal starter for a seasonal barbecue menu. Assemble the quesadillas ahead of time and cook them at the last minute. If smoked shellfish is unavailable, substitute fresh-cooked mussels, shrimp (prawns) or scallops.

TO MAKE THE SALSA, bring a saucepan three-fourths full of water to a boil. Add the corn kernels and cook for 1 minute. Drain and let cool. In a bowl, combine the corn, cilantro, green onions, lime juice and chili pepper. Mix well and season to taste with salt and pepper. You should have about 2½ cups (15 oz/470 g). Set aside.

To make the quesadillas, in a bowl, combine the shellfish, green onions and Jack, mozzarella and Cheddar cheeses. Toss to mix. Distribute the mixture evenly over 3 tortillas and top with the remaining 3 tortillas.

Place a nonstick frying pan over medium heat. When hot, add the tortillas and cook on the first side until the cheese begins to melt, 2–3 minutes. Turn and cook on the second side until the cheese is melted throughout, 2–3 minutes longer.

Transfer to a cutting board and cut each quesadilla into 6 wedges. Place on a serving plate and serve with the salsa. *Serves 6*

Fettuccine with Golden Tomatoes and Bread Crumbs

1   cup (2 oz/60 g) very coarse fresh bread crumbs

2   tablespoons extra-virgin olive oil

     salt and freshly ground pepper

¾   lb (375 g) dried fettuccine

     fresh tomato sauce *(recipe on page 16),* made with yellow tomatoes

½   cup (2 oz/60 g) freshly grated Parmesan cheese

Wedges of large yellow tomatoes or halved yellow pear-shaped cherry tomatoes make an attractive and tasty addition to this dish. Just before serving the pasta, mix the tomatoes with 1 tablespoon extra-virgin olive oil in a frying pan over high heat and stir constantly until warm, 1–2 minutes. Then toss with the hot pasta and fresh tomato sauce.

PREHEAT AN OVEN to 375°F (190°C).

Spread the bread crumbs on a baking sheet. Drizzle with the olive oil and toss to distribute the oil evenly. Season to taste with salt and pepper. Bake, tossing occasionally, until golden brown, 8–10 minutes. Remove from the oven and let cool.

Bring a large pot three-fourths full of salted water to a rolling boil over high heat. Add the pasta, stir well and cook until al dente (tender but firm to the bite), 10–12 minutes or according to the package directions.

Meanwhile, heat the tomato sauce in a saucepan over medium-high heat, stirring occasionally, until hot, 3–5 minutes.

When the pasta is done, drain and transfer to a warmed serving bowl. Pour on the tomato sauce, toss well and season to taste with salt and pepper. Toss the bread crumbs with the Parmesan cheese and sprinkle over the top. Serve immediately. *Serves 6*

Risotto with Oven-Dried Tomatoes and Basil

1½ lb (750 g) ripe but firm plum (Roma) tomatoes

1 teaspoon kosher salt

3 cups (24 fl oz/750 ml) chicken stock

3 cups (24 fl oz/750 ml) water

1½ cups (9 oz/280 g) peeled, seeded and chopped tomatoes *(see technique, page 15)*

3 tablespoons extra-virgin olive oil

1 yellow onion, finely chopped

1½ cups (10½ oz/330 g) Arborio rice

1½ tablespoons balsamic vinegar

2 cloves garlic, finely chopped

3 tablespoons finely chopped fresh flat-leaf (Italian) parsley

salt and freshly ground pepper

20 fresh basil leaves, cut into thin strips, or basil sprigs for garnish

Oven-drying is an excellent way to prolong the shelf life of a bumper crop of tomatoes. Plum tomatoes are the best choice because their flesh is dense. Once dried, they can be stored in a cool, dark place for up to 7 days or frozen for up to 2 months. Purchased dried tomatoes can be substituted in this recipe; use 3 ounces (90 g) and add them just before the risotto is removed from the heat.

CORE THE WHOLE TOMATOES and cut in half lengthwise. Place, cut sides up, on a baking sheet and sprinkle with the kosher salt. Let stand, uncovered, for 1 hour.

Preheat an oven to 275°F (135°C). Bake the tomatoes until dry, yet still soft and plump, 5–6 hours. Let cool, then set aside.

In a saucepan, combine the stock, water and chopped tomatoes and bring to a boil. Reduce the heat to low and maintain a gentle simmer.

In a large, heavy frying pan over medium heat, warm the olive oil. Add the onion and sauté, stirring, until soft, about 10 minutes. Add the rice and stir constantly until the edges of the grains are translucent, about 4 minutes.

Increase the heat to medium-high, add a ladleful of the simmering stock mixture and cook, stirring constantly. When the liquid is almost fully absorbed, add another ladleful. Stir steadily to keep the rice from sticking and continue to add more liquid, a ladleful at a time, as soon as each previous ladleful is almost absorbed. The risotto is done when it is creamy and the rice is tender but firm, 20–25 minutes total. If you run out of stock before the rice is tender, use hot water.

Remove the risotto from the heat, cover and let stand for 5 minutes. Stir in 1 ladleful stock (or water), the vinegar, garlic, parsley and oven-dried tomatoes. Season to taste with salt and pepper. Transfer to a large warmed platter or individual shallow bowls and garnish with basil. Serve immediately. *Serves 6*

Figs, Prosciutto and St.-André Cheese

⅓ cup (3 fl oz/80 ml) crème fraîche

2 teaspoons chopped fresh mint, plus mint sprigs for garnish

2 teaspoons fresh lemon juice

2–3 teaspoons milk

salt and freshly ground pepper

12 ripe figs, a single variety or a mixture *(see note)*

6 oz (185 g) St.-André or other triple-cream cheese such as Explorateur, cut into 12 wedges

3 oz (90 g) thinly sliced prosciutto

Figs were brought to North America by the Spanish missionaries who came to California to build a network of Catholic missions. They found the climate particularly favorable to growing figs, which resulted in the naming of the purple-black variety known as the Black Mission. Other figs can be used for this recipe, including the large, fat, white-fleshed, green-skinned Calimyrna, and the small, thick-skinned, green Kadota. Or consider an assortment of all three.

IN A SMALL BOWL, whisk together the crème fraîche, chopped mint, lemon juice and as much of the milk as needed to form a thick, creamy consistency. Season to taste with salt and pepper.

Halve the figs and arrange them on individual plates or a platter. Intersperse the wedges of cheese among the figs. Drape the prosciutto around the figs and drizzle with the crème fraîche mixture. Garnish with mint sprigs and serve. *Serves 6*

Flat Bread with Tomato, Mozzarella and Basil Salad

For the flat bread:

1   package (2½ teaspoons) active dry yeast

¾   cup (6 fl oz/180 ml) luke-warm water (110°F/43°C)

2   cups (10 oz/315 g) all-purpose (plain) flour, plus flour as needed

¾   teaspoon salt

3   tablespoons extra-virgin olive oil

For the salad:

1½ tablespoons extra-virgin olive oil

1½ tablespoons balsamic vinegar

1   clove garlic, minced

    salt and freshly ground pepper

¾   lb (375 g) cherry tomatoes, stemmed and halved (*see note*)

1   ball fresh mozzarella cheese, about 6 oz (185 g), quartered and then sliced ¼ inch (6 mm) thick

½   cup (½ oz/15 g) loosely packed fresh small basil leaves

Any color cherry tomato can be used—yellow, red, green or orange—alone or a mixture. If you like, substitute 14 ounces (440 g) thawed frozen store-bought pizza dough for the flat bread dough.

TO MAKE THE FLAT BREAD, in a large bowl, combine the yeast, ¼ cup (2 fl oz/60 ml) of the lukewarm water and ¼ cup (1½ oz/45 g) of the flour. Let stand until bubbly and slightly risen, about 20 minutes. Add the remaining 1¾ cups (8½ oz/270 g) flour, the salt, olive oil and the remaining ½ cup (4 fl oz/120 ml) water and mix well. When the dough comes together into a ball, transfer it to a lightly floured work surface. Knead until soft, smooth and elastic, about 10 minutes, adding flour as needed to prevent sticking. Place in an oiled bowl and turn the dough to oil the top. Cover the bowl with plastic wrap and let the dough rise in a warm place until doubled in bulk, about 1 hour.

Meanwhile, position a rack in the bottom part of an oven and place a pizza stone on it, or line with unglazed quarry tiles. Set the oven temperature to 500°F (260°C) and preheat for 30 minutes.

Punch down the dough and transfer to a lightly floured work surface. Roll out into an oval 9 by 13 inches (23 by 33 cm) in diameter and ½ inch (12 mm) thick. Transfer to a flour-dusted pizza peel or rimless baking sheet, then slide the dough onto the heated stone or tiles. Bake until golden and crisp, 8–10 minutes. Using the pizza peel or baking sheet, transfer to a cutting board. Cut into 6 pieces and arrange them on a platter.

To make the salad, in a large bowl, whisk together the olive oil, balsamic vinegar, garlic and salt and pepper to taste. Add the tomatoes and mozzarella and carefully mix together. Spoon the salad atop the flat bread and garnish with the basil. Serve immediately. *Serves 6*

Corn and Red Pepper Fritters with Red Pepper Coulis

1   **cup (5 oz/155 g) all-purpose (plain) flour**

½   **teaspoon salt, plus salt to taste**

2   **eggs, separated**

2   **tablespoons olive oil**

¾   **cup (6 fl oz/180 ml) flat beer, at room temperature**

5   **red bell peppers (capsicums)**

6   **tablespoons (3 fl oz/90 ml) heavy (double) cream**

2   **tablespoons sour cream**

1   **teaspoon balsamic vinegar**

     cayenne pepper and freshly ground black pepper

     canola oil for frying

2   **cups (12 oz/375 g) corn kernels (from 3 ears)** *(see note)*

⅓   **cup (½ oz/15 g) snipped fresh chives**

For this recipe, you can use corncobs with small, white kernels, fuller-bodied yellow kernels, or the hybrid Butter and Sugar corn, which sports both colors.

IN A BOWL, sift together the flour and the ½ teaspoon salt. Make a well in the center. In a small bowl, beat the egg yolks and add to the well along with the olive oil and beer. Whisk well to form a batter. Let stand at room temperature for 1 hour.

Preheat a broiler (griller). Cut each bell pepper in half lengthwise and remove the stem, seeds and ribs. Place, cut sides down, on a baking sheet and broil (grill) until the skins are blackened and blistered. Remove from the broiler and cover loosely with aluminum foil. Let steam for about 10 minutes, then peel off the skins. Finely dice 4 of the pepper halves and set aside.

To make the coulis, place the remaining peppers in a blender and purée until smooth. In a bowl, combine the heavy cream and sour cream and mix well. Add the pepper purée and whisk until the cream thickens slightly. Add the vinegar and season to taste with cayenne pepper, salt and black pepper. Cover and refrigerate until needed.

Pour canola oil into a deep, heavy sauté pan to a depth of 1 inch (2.5 cm). Heat to 375°F (190°C) on a deep-frying thermometer.

Meanwhile, add the corn, diced peppers, chives and salt and black pepper to taste to the prepared batter. Using a whisk or an electric mixer, beat the egg whites until stiff peaks form. Using a rubber spatula, fold the whites into the batter just until no white drifts remain.

Working in batches, drop the batter by heaping tablespoonfuls into the oil; do not crowd the pan. Cook, turning once, until golden brown, 1–2 minutes total. Using a slotted spoon, transfer to paper towels to drain briefly, then arrange on a warmed platter. Drizzle the coulis over the fritters or place in a bowl alongside. Serve hot. *Makes about 24 fritters; serves 6*

Linguine with Pesto and Borage Flowers

1   **teaspoon extra-virgin olive oil**

¼   **cup (1¼ oz/37 g) pine nuts**

1   **lb (500 g) dried linguine or fettuccine**

    basil pesto *(recipe on page 16)*

    small handful borage flowers, optional

Borage flourishes in the countries surrounding the Mediterranean. Its green-gray leaves have a velvety texture, and its star-shaped purple flowers are sweet with nectar. Always add the flowers to dishes at the last moment to retain their vivid color. Borage blossoms offer a lovely blaze of purple and a light peppery flavor to this dish, but any variety of edible summer blossoms will accomplish the same effect. Nasturtiums are an especially good alternative.

IN A FRYING PAN over medium heat, warm the olive oil. Add the pine nuts and cook, stirring constantly, until a light golden brown, 3–4 minutes. Remove from the heat and set aside.

Bring a large pot three-fourths full of salted water to a rolling boil over high heat. Add the pasta, stir well and cook until al dente (tender but firm to the bite), 10–12 minutes or according to the package directions.

When the pasta is done, scoop out ¼ cup (2 fl oz/60 ml) of the pasta water and set aside. Immediately drain the pasta and transfer to a large bowl.

Add the pasta water, pesto and pine nuts to the pasta and toss well. Transfer to a warmed serving bowl, garnish with the borage flowers, if desired, and serve immediately. *Serves 6*

Too many flowers...too little fruit.

—Sir Walter Scott

Stuffed Zucchini Flowers

24   zucchini (courgette) flowers

2   cups (16 fl oz/500 ml) water,
     or as needed

1⅔   cups (9 oz/280 g) all-purpose
     (plain) flour, or as needed

½   teaspoon salt, plus salt to
     taste

⅛   teaspoon freshly ground
     pepper

6   anchovy fillets packed in
     olive oil, drained and
     chopped

     olive oil for frying

10   oz (315 g) fresh mozzarella
     cheese, diced

     lemon wedges

Male zucchini flowers, which are those without the immature squash attached, are generally preferred for stuffing. Select blossoms that are bright orange, unbruised and wide open. They are highly perishable, so cook them the same day they are picked or purchased.

DETACH THE GREEN STEMS and leaves from the zucchini flowers and gently remove any pistils. Wash the flowers quickly under cold running water and dry gently with paper towels.

Pour the 2 cups (16 fl oz/500 ml) water into a bowl. In another bowl, sift together the flour, the ½ teaspoon salt and the pepper. Then sift the flour mixture into the water while stirring constantly. The batter should be the consistency of thick heavy (double) cream. If it is too thin, add additional flour; if it is too thick, add additional water. Let stand for 30 minutes.

Meanwhile, place the anchovies in a small bowl and add water to cover; let soak for 10 minutes, then drain.

Pour olive oil into a deep, heavy sauté pan to a depth of 1 inch (2.5 cm). Heat to 375°F (190°C) on a deep-frying thermometer.

Meanwhile, make the filling: In a small bowl, combine the mozzarella and anchovies. Carefully open the flowers and fill each one with an equal portion of the filling. Twist the petals together slightly to close the tops.

When the oil is ready, dip a few of the flowers into the batter and slip them into the oil; do not crowd the pan. Deep-fry, turning once, until golden and crisp, 1–2 minutes total. Using a slotted spoon, transfer to paper towels to drain briefly. Repeat with the remaining flowers.

Arrange the flowers on a platter or individual plates. Sprinkle with salt to taste. Garnish with lemon wedges and serve immediately. *Serves 6*

soups
and salads

Golden Gazpacho

1   slice coarse white bread

3   lb (1.5 kg) yellow tomatoes, peeled, seeded and chopped

1   green bell pepper (capsicum), seeded, deribbed and chopped

1   red (Spanish) onion, coarsely chopped

1   large English (hothouse) cucumber, peeled and coarsely chopped

6   tablespoons (3 fl oz/90 ml) red wine vinegar

3   large cloves garlic, minced

1¼ cups (10 fl oz/310 ml) tomato juice

3   tablespoons extra-virgin olive oil

For the garnish:

1   tablespoon unsalted butter

1   tablespoon olive oil

3   cloves garlic, crushed

6   slices coarse white bread, crusts removed, cut into small cubes

    salt and freshly ground pepper

¼   cup (1¼ oz/37 g) diced green bell pepper (capsicum)

¼   cup (1¼ oz/37 g) peeled, seeded and diced cucumber

¼   cup (1 oz/30 g) diced red (Spanish) onion

1½ cups (9 oz/280 g) red cherry tomatoes, quartered

In Spain, there are over 30 distinct versions of the famed cold soup known as gazpacho. It was first introduced in southern Spain by the Moors, who originally made it with garlic, bread, olive oil, lemon, water and salt. When the tomato was introduced to Spanish cooks in the early 16th century, gazpacho took on its familiar rosy hue. Yellow tomatoes give this version of the soup its marvelous golden color.

REMOVE THE CRUST from the bread slice and place in a shallow bowl with water to cover. Let stand until the bread is fully soaked, then remove and squeeze dry. In a bowl, combine the soaked bread, yellow tomatoes, bell pepper, onion, cucumber, vinegar, garlic, tomato juice and olive oil. Stir well. Working in batches, transfer the mixture to a blender and process on high speed until very smooth, about 3 minutes for each batch. Strain through a coarse-mesh sieve into a clean bowl. Cover and chill for 1 hour.

To prepare the garnish, in a frying pan over medium heat, melt the butter with the olive oil. Add the garlic and cook, stirring, until golden brown, about 1 minute. Remove the garlic and discard. Add the bread cubes, and stir to coat with the butter and oil. Cook slowly, stirring occasionally, until golden, 10–12 minutes. Remove the croutons from the heat and let cool.

Before serving, season the soup to taste with salt and pepper. Ladle the soup into chilled individual bowls and garnish each serving with bell pepper, cucumber, onion, cherry tomatoes and croutons. Serve well chilled. *Serves 6*

He had been eight years upon a project for extracting sunbeams out of cucumbers, which were to be put in vials heremetically sealed, and let out to warm the air in raw inclement summers.

—Jonathan Swift

Chilled Cucumber Soup

3   **cups (1½ lb/750 g) plain yogurt**

1   **large English (hothouse) cucumber, peeled, halved, seeded and coarsely grated, plus 6 paper-thin cucumber slices with skin intact for garnish**

2   **cloves garlic, minced**

1   **tablespoon extra-virgin olive oil**

1½   **tablespoons chopped fresh mint**

2½   **tablespoons chopped fresh dill, plus 6 dill sprigs for garnish**

2   **cups (16 fl oz/500 ml) milk**

3   **tablespoons white wine vinegar or fresh lemon juice**

   salt and freshly ground pepper

Cucumbers are native to Asia, where they have been eaten for thousands of years. They contain a great deal of water, which makes them particularly refreshing in the hot summer months. When choosing cucumbers, avoid the waxed variety sold in grocery stores year-round, and instead seek out the long, thin-skinned English or hothouse variety. It has a superior flavor, less water and far fewer seeds. Three lemon cucumbers can be substituted for the single English (hothouse) cucumber, if you like.

LINE A SIEVE with cheesecloth (muslin) and place over a large bowl. Spoon the yogurt into the sieve and let drain in the refrigerator for 4 hours. Discard the captured liquid and place the yogurt in the bowl.

Add the grated cucumber, garlic, olive oil, mint, chopped dill and milk. Mix well. Stir in the vinegar or lemon juice. Cover and chill for 1 hour.

Before serving, season to taste with salt and pepper. Ladle the soup into chilled individual bowls and garnish each serving with a cucumber slice and a dill sprig. Serve well chilled. *Serves 6*

Summer Vegetable Soup with Basil-Mint Pesto

½   **cup (3½ oz/105 g) dried small white (navy) beans**

2   **tablespoons extra-virgin olive oil**

1   **small yellow onion, chopped**

2   **small carrots, peeled and diced**

2   **small celery stalks, diced**

2   **cups (12 oz/375 g) peeled, seeded and chopped tomatoes** *(see technique, page 15)*

4   **cups (32 fl oz/1 l) chicken stock or vegetable stock**

3   **cups (24 fl oz/750 ml) water**

½   **lb (250 g) green beans, trimmed and cut on the diagonal into 1-inch (2.5-cm) lengths**

¼   **lb (125 g) dried penne or small elbow pasta**

3   **cups (3 oz/90 g) loosely packed Swiss chard (silver-beet) leaves (about 1 small bunch), coarsely chopped**

    salt and freshly ground pepper

½   **recipe basil-mint pesto** *(recipe on page 16)*

⅓   **cup (1½ oz/45 g) freshly grated Parmesan cheese**

A traditional basil pesto laced with mint brings out the fresh flavors of this hearty soup. Spoon it directly onto the top of each bowl just before serving, or pass it at the table for guests to help themselves.

PICK OVER THE WHITE BEANS and discard any damaged beans or stones. Rinse well and place in a bowl with water to cover generously. Let soak for 3 hours. Drain and place in a saucepan with water to cover by 2 inches (5 cm). Bring to a boil, reduce the heat to low and simmer gently, uncovered, until slightly tender, 30–40 minutes. Drain, discarding the liquid. Set the beans aside.

In a large soup pot over medium-low heat, warm the olive oil. Add the onion, carrots and celery and cook uncovered, stirring occasionally, until the vegetables are soft, about 20 minutes. Add the tomatoes, stock, water and drained white beans and continue to cook, uncovered, until the beans are very tender and quite soft, about 45 minutes longer.

About 15 minutes before the beans are ready, add the green beans and pasta. Cover and simmer until the pasta is tender to the bite, 8–10 minutes. Add the Swiss chard and cook until it wilts, about 2 minutes. Season to taste with salt and pepper.

Ladle the soup into warmed individual bowls and place a large spoonful of the pesto on top of each serving. Sprinkle with the Parmesan and serve immediately. *Serves 6*

Cool Honeydew-Mint Soup

½ large honeydew melon, 2 lb (1 kg), seeded, peeled and cut into pieces

¼ cup (¼ oz/7 g) loosely packed fresh mint leaves, plus mint sprigs for garnish

3 tablespoons fresh lime juice, or as needed

1 tablespoon honey

salt

paper-thin lime slices

Melons thrive in warm climates during the summer months. The honeydew melon, available both with green skin and flesh and with yellow skin and orange flesh, is principally grown in the hot reaches of the Mediterranean, Africa, the Caribbean, Central and South America, and California. Casaba, Crenshaw, Persian or cantaloupe melons can be substituted with equally pleasing results.

WORKING IN BATCHES, place the melon, mint leaves, 3 tablespoons lime juice, and honey in a blender. Process on high speed until smooth and light, about 2 minutes for each batch.

Transfer to a container, cover and chill for at least 1 hour.

Before serving, season to taste with more lime juice, if needed, and salt. Ladle the soup into chilled individual bowls and garnish with lime slices and mint sprigs. Serve well chilled. *Serves 6*

Spicy Grilled Chicken Salad with Peppers and Tomatoes

4	skinless, boneless chicken breast halves, about 6 oz (185 g) each
1	tablespoon olive oil
2	red, green, yellow or orange bell peppers (capsicums), or a mixture, seeded, deribbed and very thinly sliced
1	fresh pasilla chili pepper, seeded and very thinly sliced
½	fresh jalapeño pepper, seeded and minced
1	small red (Spanish) onion, thinly sliced
	salt and freshly ground pepper
2	cloves garlic, minced
½	teaspoon red pepper flakes
3	tablespoons red wine vinegar
2	tablespoons balsamic vinegar
5	tablespoons (2½ fl oz/75 ml) extra-virgin olive oil
½	lb (250 g) assorted cherry tomatoes such as red, yellow, green, orange and yellow pear, halved
½	cup (2½ oz/75 g) brine-cured black olives, preferably Niçoise or Kalamata
40	fresh small basil leaves

In Italy, this salad is called *pollo forte,* meaning "strong chicken," a name derived from the fiery hot peppers that season the bird. The amount of heat is up to you: add or subtract the chili peppers as you wish. The salad serves six as a light first course or as an accompaniment to a bowl of chilled gazpacho *(recipe on page 40).* As a luncheon main course, the recipe serves four.

PREPARE A FIRE in a charcoal grill.

Brush the chicken breasts with the 1 tablespoon olive oil. Place the chicken breasts on the grill rack about 4 inches (10 cm) from the fire and grill until golden brown on the first side, 4–5 minutes. Turn the chicken and continue to grill until golden brown on the second side and opaque in the center, 4–5 minutes longer. Transfer to a cutting board and let cool for 20 minutes, then cut across the grain into very thin strips.

Place the chicken strips in a large bowl and add the bell, pasilla and jalapeño peppers and the onion. Mix well and season to taste with salt and pepper. Cover and refrigerate until needed.

In a small bowl, whisk together the garlic, red pepper flakes, red wine vinegar, balsamic vinegar and extra-virgin olive oil. Season to taste with salt and pepper. Pour over the chicken mixture, toss to mix and return to the refrigerator for 15 minutes.

To serve, add the cherry tomatoes, olives and basil to the chicken mixture. Toss well and transfer to a serving bowl or individual plates. Serve chilled or at room temperature. *Serves 6*

Bread Salad with Tomatoes and Lemon Cucumbers

3   lemon cucumbers or 1 English (hothouse) cucumber, peeled, halved, seeded and diced

coarse salt

½   lb (250 g) stale coarse-textured white bread *(see note)*

½   cup (4 fl oz/125 ml) water

5   ripe tomatoes, 1½–2 lb (750 g–1 kg) total, seeded and diced

1   red (Spanish) onion, diced

4–5 tablespoons (2–2½ fl oz/ 60–80 ml) red wine vinegar

⅓   cup (3 fl oz/80 ml) extra-virgin olive oil

salt and freshly ground pepper

½   cup (½ oz/15 g) loosely packed fresh basil leaves, torn into small pieces

This rustic Tuscan salad, called *panzanella,* is best when made with a chewy, coarsely textured white bread. The bread must be at least 3 to 4 days old to provide the correct texture when mixed with tomatoes and vinaigrette. Round, yellow lemon cucumbers deliver a sweet, mild flavor to the salad.

SPREAD THE DICED CUCUMBERS on paper towels and sprinkle with coarse salt. Let stand for 15 minutes. Place the cucumbers in a colander and rinse with cold water. Pat dry with paper towels.

Meanwhile, cut the bread into slices 1 inch (2.5 cm) thick and place in a shallow dish. Sprinkle the bread with the water and let stand for 2 minutes. Then carefully squeeze the bread until it is dry. Tear into rough 1-inch (2.5-cm) pieces and place on paper towels. Let stand for 10 minutes.

In a bowl, combine the cucumbers, tomatoes, onion and bread; toss gently.

In a large bowl, whisk together the vinegar and olive oil. Season to taste with salt and pepper. Add the bread mixture and the basil, mix gently and refrigerate for at least 1 hour, or for up to 4 hours.

Transfer to a platter and serve chilled. *Serves 4–6*

Green Garden Salad with Summer Flowers

¼   **baguette, thinly sliced on the diagonal**

6   **tablespoons (3 fl oz/90 ml) extra-virgin olive oil**

2   **cloves garlic**

2   **tablespoons balsamic vinegar**

1½   **teaspoons red wine vinegar**

1   **shallot, minced**

    salt and freshly ground pepper

9   **cups (9 oz/280 g) loosely packed salad greens *(see note)*, carefully rinsed and dried**

¾   **cup (¾ oz/20 g) assorted pesticide-free edible flowers such as nasturtiums, pansies, borage and rose petals, carefully rinsed and dried**

All kinds of summer garden lettuces can be gathered for this salad. In the south of France, this combination is called *mesclun,* Provençal dialect for "mixed," and generally refers to an assortment of young shoots and plants. Traditionally the greens were picked wild, but today there are a myriad of wonderful seedlings sold for planting at home, and a broad range of young, tender greens available at farmers' markets and greengrocers. Try a mixture of frisée, mâche, lamb's lettuce, Bibb (Boston) lettuce, garden cress and red leaf.

PREHEAT AN OVEN to 350°F (180°C).

Brush the baguette slices on both sides with 2 tablespoons of the olive oil and place in a single layer on a baking sheet. Bake until crisp and lightly golden, 8–10 minutes. Remove from the oven. When cool enough to handle, lightly rub the toasts on both sides with the garlic cloves. Set aside.

In a small bowl, whisk together the remaining 4 tablespoons (2 fl oz/ 60 ml) olive oil, the balsamic vinegar, red wine vinegar, shallot and salt and pepper to taste to make a vinaigrette.

To serve, place the greens in a large salad bowl and drizzle with the vinaigrette. Toss well and garnish with the flowers. Serve with the toasts on the side. *Serves 6*

I came to love my rows, my beans . . . They attached me to the earth, and so I got strength . . .

—Henry David Thoreau

Pasta Salad with Summer Beans and Herbs

¾ **lb (375 g) dried fusilli**

6 **tablespoons (3 fl oz/90 ml) extra-virgin olive oil**

1 **lb (500 g) assorted snap beans such as green, yellow and haricot vert, trimmed**

2 **lb (1 kg) fresh shell beans of choice, shelled** *(see note)*

5 **tablespoons (3 fl oz/80 ml) red wine vinegar**

2 **cloves garlic, minced**

2 **tablespoons chopped fresh flat-leaf (Italian) parsley, plus parsley sprigs for garnish**

1 **tablespoon chopped fresh mint, plus mint sprigs for garnish**

2 **teaspoons chopped fresh oregano, plus oregano sprigs for garnish**

 salt and freshly ground pepper

Shell beans can be found fresh in the late summer months, before the pods begin to show signs of drying. Because most shell beans, such as the kidney, cannellini, scarlet runner, lima, cranberry and black-eyed pea varieties, are used dry, few cooks realize the distinctive quality they add when included fresh in summer dishes. Select any type you like for this recipe.

BRING A LARGE POT three-fourths full of salted water to a rolling boil over high heat. Add the fusilli, stir well and boil until al dente (tender but firm to the bite), 12–15 minutes or according to the package directions. Drain and transfer to a large bowl. Immediately add 1 tablespoon of the olive oil and toss well. Cover and place in the refrigerator to cool.

Refill the pot three-fourths full with salted water and bring to a boil over high heat. Add the snap beans and boil until tender, 4–6 minutes. Drain and rinse under cold water to halt the cooking. Add to the pasta in the refrigerator.

Again refill the pot three-fourths full with salted water and bring to a boil over high heat. Add the shell beans and boil until tender, 5–10 minutes, depending upon the variety. Drain, add to the pasta and snap beans; let cool completely in the refrigerator for at least 1 hour or for up to 24 hours.

In a large bowl, whisk together the remaining 5 tablespoons (3 fl oz/80 ml) olive oil, the vinegar and garlic. Pour over the pasta and beans and add the chopped parsley, mint and oregano. Toss together well. Season to taste with salt and pepper.

To serve, transfer the salad to a large serving dish and garnish with parsley, mint and oregano sprigs. *Serves 6*

Creamy Potato Salad

3   lb (1.5 kg) red potatoes, unpeeled

⅓   cup (2½ oz/75 g) plain yogurt

¼   cup (2 fl oz/60 ml) mayonnaise

¼   cup (2 fl oz/60 ml) sour cream

1   tablespoon Dijon mustard

3   tablespoons fresh lemon juice

8   green (spring) onions, thinly sliced

2   celery stalks, finely chopped

3   tablespoons chopped fresh flat-leaf (Italian) parsley, plus parsley sprigs for garnish

3   tablespoons chopped fresh mint, plus mint sprigs for garnish

3   tablespoons chopped fresh basil, plus basil sprigs for garnish

    salt and freshly ground pepper

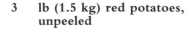

Serve this salad with a batch of your favorite barbecued ribs or chicken for an old-fashioned summer picnic. If desired, add 2 hard-cooked eggs, chopped, or ½ cup (2 oz/60 g) chopped red (Spanish) onion with the potatoes.

BRING A LARGE POT three-fourths full of salted water to a boil over high heat. Add the potatoes and boil until tender when pierced with a fork, 15–20 minutes. Drain and let cool completely in the refrigerator for at least 1 hour. Cut the potatoes into ¾-inch (2-cm) dice.

In a large bowl, stir together the yogurt, mayonnaise, sour cream, mustard, lemon juice, green onions, celery and the chopped parsley, mint and basil. Add the potatoes. Season to taste with salt and pepper and toss gently to mix.

To serve, place the salad in a large serving bowl and garnish with parsley, mint and basil sprigs. *Serves 6*

Farmers' Market Tomato Salad

1 **very small yellow onion, cut into paper-thin slices**

   salt

½ **cup (4 fl oz/125 ml) milk**

½ **cup (4 oz/125 g) plain yogurt**

1–2 **tablespoons fresh lemon juice**

1 **clove garlic, minced**

1 **tablespoon chopped fresh oregano**

1½ **tablespoons chopped fresh basil**

2 **teaspoons extra-virgin olive oil**

   freshly ground pepper

6 **ripe tomatoes, thinly sliced**

1 **English (hothouse) cucumber, peeled and cut crosswise into thin slices**

   handful of fresh basil leaves

   handful of fresh cherry tomatoes

Farmers' markets are cropping up everywhere, offering an incredible selection of fruits and vegetables. Most provide a variety of fresh red, yellow and orange summer tomatoes, all of which need little embellishment to highlight their sweet, sun-ripened flavor.

PLACE THE ONION SLICES in a bowl and sprinkle with salt. Pour the milk over the onion and let stand for 30 minutes.

Meanwhile, in a small bowl, whisk together the yogurt, lemon juice, garlic, oregano, basil, olive oil and salt and pepper to taste to form a vinaigrette. Cover and refrigerate until needed.

Arrange the tomato and cucumber slices on a plate. Drain the onion slices and pat dry with paper towels. Scatter the onions atop the tomatoes and cucumbers. Drizzle with the vinaigrette, top with the basil leaves and cherry tomatoes and serve. *Serves 6*

Salade Niçoise

2   **cloves garlic, minced**

3   **tablespoons red wine vinegar**

5   **tablespoons (2½ fl oz/75 ml) extra-virgin olive oil**

    salt and freshly ground pepper

2   **red or yellow bell peppers (capsicums), or a mixture**

¾   **lb (375 g) fingerling or small Yukon Gold potatoes, unpeeled**

¾   **lb (375 g) assorted snap beans such as green, yellow and haricot vert, trimmed**

1¼   **lb (625 g) fresh tuna steaks, about ¾ inch (2 cm) thick, cut into 6 equal pieces**

½   **lb (250 g) red or yellow cherry tomatoes or a mixture, halved**

½   **cup (2½ oz/75 g) brine-cured black olives, preferably Niçoise**

3   **hard-cooked eggs, peeled and quartered lengthwise**

3   **tablespoons drained capers**

1   **can (2 oz/60 g) anchovy fillets packed in olive oil, drained, soaked in cold water for 10 minutes, drained, patted dry and cut in half crosswise**

2   **teaspoons chopped fresh parsley**

1   **tablespoon snipped fresh chives**

1   **teaspoon chopped fresh thyme**

Different variations on this appealing salad are popular in the south of France. In this version, grilled or panfried fresh tuna is used instead of the traditional canned variety.

IF GRILLING THE TUNA, prepare a fire in a charcoal grill.

In a small bowl, whisk together the garlic, vinegar and 4 tablespoons (2 fl oz/60 ml) of the olive oil. Season to taste with salt and pepper. Set aside.

Cut each bell pepper in half lengthwise and remove the stem, seeds and ribs. Place the peppers cut sides down on a baking sheet and slip under a broiler (griller), or place cut sides up over the charcoal fire. Broil or grill until the skins are blackened and blistered. Remove from the broiler or grill and cover loosely with aluminum foil. Let steam until cool enough to handle, about 10 minutes, then peel off the skins. Cut lengthwise into strips 1 inch (2.5 cm) wide. Set aside.

Bring a large saucepan three-fourths full of salted water to a boil over high heat. Add the potatoes and boil until tender, 10–15 minutes. Using a slotted spoon, transfer to a cutting board and let cool. Add the beans to the same pan and boil until tender, 4–6 minutes. Drain and rinse under cold running water to halt the cooking. Cut the cooled potatoes lengthwise into quarters.

If grilling the tuna, brush the pieces on both sides with the remaining 1 tablespoon olive oil and place on the grill rack about 4 inches (10 cm) above the fire. If panfrying, heat the remaining 1 tablespoon olive oil in a wide frying pan over medium heat, then add the tuna. Grill or panfry, turning once, until golden on the outside but still slightly pink at the center, 3–4 minutes on each side, or until done to your liking. Season to taste with salt and pepper.

To serve, arrange the tuna, potatoes and beans on a platter or individual plates. Garnish with the pepper strips, tomatoes, olives, eggs, capers and anchovies. Drizzle with the vinaigrette and sprinkle with the herbs. *Serves 6*

Couscous Salad with Grilled Summer Vegetables

2½ cups (20 fl oz/625 ml) water

1¼ cups (6½ oz/200 g) couscous

2 bell peppers (capsicums) *(see note)*

1 red or green chili pepper such as serrano or jalapeño

1 Asian (slender) eggplant (aubergine), cut crosswise into slices

1 zucchini (courgette), cut crosswise into slices

7 tablespoons (3½ fl oz/105 ml) extra-virgin olive oil

2 large red tomatoes, diced

2 tablespoons chopped fresh flat-leaf (Italian) parsley

⅓ cup (½ oz/15 g) chopped fresh cilantro (fresh coriander), plus cilantro sprigs for garnish

6 tablespoons (3 fl oz/90 ml) fresh lemon juice

1 teaspoon ground cumin

3 cloves garlic, minced

   salt and freshly ground pepper

6 lemon wedges

If your garden or farmers' market has orange or purple bell peppers, use them for this colorful salad; otherwise red, yellow or green bell peppers will do. For a heartier dish, add ¾ pound (375 g) grilled shrimp (prawns) or grilled chicken, cut into strips, with the tomatoes.

IN A SAUCEPAN, bring the water to a boil. Add the couscous, cover, remove from the heat and let stand for 10 minutes. Dump the couscous onto a paper towel–lined baking sheet, spread it out, and let stand at room temperature for 30 minutes. Transfer to a bowl, cover and chill for 30 minutes.

Meanwhile, prepare a fire in a charcoal grill.

Cut each bell pepper and the chili pepper in half lengthwise and remove the stems, seeds and ribs. Place the bell pepper and chili halves, cut sides up, on the grill rack and grill until the skins are blackened and blistered. Remove from the grill and cover loosely with aluminum foil. Let steam until cool enough to handle, about 10 minutes, then peel off the skins. Cut the bell pepper into 1-inch (2.5-cm) squares and mince the jalapeño. Add to the couscous.

While the peppers are steaming, brush the eggplant and zucchini slices on both sides with 2 tablespoons of the olive oil and place on the grill rack. Grill, turning occasionally, until golden brown and tender when pierced with a fork, 6–8 minutes for the zucchini and 8–12 minutes for the eggplant. Add to the couscous along with the tomatoes, parsley and chopped cilantro.

In a small bowl, whisk together the remaining 5 tablespoons (3 fl oz/80 ml) olive oil, the lemon juice, cumin, garlic and salt and pepper to taste. Drizzle over the couscous and vegetables and toss to mix.

Transfer the salad to a serving platter and garnish with the lemon wedges and cilantro sprigs. *Serves 6*

main
courses

Barbecued Chicken

6   chicken breast halves, about ½ lb (250 g) each, excess fat removed

6   chicken drumsticks, about ¼ lb (125 g) each, excess fat removed

6   chicken thighs, 5–6 oz (155–185 g) each, excess fat removed

     salt and freshly ground pepper

     barbecue sauce *(recipe on page 17) (see note)*

Serve this summertime classic with chili-rubbed corn on the cob *(recipe on page 104)* and creamy potato salad *(page 56)*. To give the sauce an even spicier edge, add 1 teaspoon each ground cumin and paprika and 1 tablespoon chili powder with the allspice and ginger.

PREPARE A FIRE in a charcoal grill.

Sprinkle the chicken pieces with salt and pepper on all sides and place them, skin side down, on the grill rack about 6 inches (15 cm) from the fire. Grill, turning frequently, until well browned on all sides, 20–25 minutes. If the fire flares up, spritz with water from a spray bottle. If the chicken pieces are getting too dark, place them around the perimeter of the grill rack over less direct heat.

After 20–25 minutes, brush the chicken with the sauce and cook for another 5 minutes. Turn over the pieces, brush with more sauce and continue to cook until the chicken is no longer pink when cut at the bone, about 5 minutes longer.

To serve, place the chicken on a warmed platter. Pass the remaining sauce at the table. *Serves 6*

Beef is a pleasure food, and we deserve pleasure.

—Jim Harrison

Grilled Flank Steak with Gorgonzola Butter

For the butter:

3   tablespoons unsalted butter, at room temperature

3   oz (90 g) Gorgonzola cheese, at room temperature

2   green (spring) onions, minced

1   tablespoon chopped fresh flat-leaf (Italian) parsley

    salt and freshly ground pepper

1   flank steak, about 2½ lb (1.25 kg), trimmed of excess fat

Grilled flank steak is perfect for summer entertaining. If you like, you can make the butter up to a few days in advance so that the only task that remains is grilling the steak. Serve with grilled "thick-slice" red onions *(recipe on page 103)* and grilled Yukon Gold potatoes with garlic and herbs *(page 99)*.

PREPARE A FIRE in a charcoal grill.

While the coals are heating, make the butter: In a bowl, using a fork, mash together the butter and Gorgonzola. Add the green onions and parsley and continue to mash until well mixed. Season to taste with salt and pepper. Mound the mixture in the center of a large piece of plastic wrap. Drape one side of the plastic wrap over the mixture and roll the butter into a sausage shape about 1½ inches (4 cm) in diameter. Wrap completely in the plastic wrap and twist the ends to seal. Refrigerate until ready to serve.

Place the steak on the grill rack about 4 inches (10 cm) from the fire and grill on the first side until browned, about 5 minutes. Season the meat with salt and pepper, turn and continue to grill until browned on the second side, 5–6 minutes longer, or until an instant-read meat thermometer inserted into the thickest part of the steak registers 135°F (57°C) for medium-rare or until done to your liking. Remove from the grill and transfer to a cutting board. Cover loosely with aluminum foil and let stand for 10 minutes before carving.

To serve, cut the meat on the diagonal and across the grain into thin slices. Arrange the meat slices on a warmed platter. Cut the butter into thin slices and place them on top of the meat and between the slices, distributing them evenly. Serve immediately. *Serves 6*

A happy soul, that all the way
To heaven hath a summer's day.

—Richard Crashaw

Summer Vegetable Calzone

For the dough:

1	package (2½ teaspoons) active dry yeast
1	cup (8 fl oz/250 ml) luke-warm water (110°F/43°C)
3	cups (15 oz/470 g) all-purpose (plain) flour, plus flour as needed
¾	teaspoon salt
3	tablespoons extra-virgin olive oil

For the filling:

5	Asian (slender) eggplants, 1 lb (500 g) total, cut on the diagonal into thin slices
3	tablespoons extra-virgin olive oil
	salt and freshly ground pepper
2	red bell peppers (capsicums), seeded, deribbed and cut lengthwise into narrow strips
2	tablespoons balsamic vinegar
¼	cup (1¼ oz/37 g) pine nuts
20	large fresh basil leaves, coarsely chopped, plus basil sprigs for garnish
1½	cups (6 oz/185 g) shredded Fontina cheese
1½	cups (6 oz/185 g) shredded mozzarella cheese
¾	cup (4 oz/125 g) crumbled goat cheese

TO MAKE THE DOUGH, in a large bowl, combine the yeast, ¼ cup (2 fl oz/60 ml) of the lukewarm water and ¼ cup (1½ oz/45 g) of the flour. Let stand until bubbly and slightly risen, about 20 minutes. Add the remaining flour, the salt, oil and the remaining water and mix with a wooden spoon until the dough comes together into a ball. Transfer to a floured surface and knead until smooth and elastic, about 10 minutes, adding flour as needed to prevent sticking. Place in an oiled bowl and turn the dough to oil the top. Cover with plastic wrap and let rise in a warm place until doubled in bulk, about 1 hour.

Meanwhile, position a rack in the top part of an oven and preheat to 400°F (200°C).

To make the filling, brush the eggplant slices on both sides with 2 table-spoons of the olive oil. Place on a baking sheet and bake, turning once, until golden and tender, 15–20 minutes. Season to taste with salt and pepper; set aside.

Position the rack in the bottom part of the oven and place a pizza stone on it, or line with unglazed quarry tiles. Raise the oven temperature to 500°F (260°C) and preheat for 30 minutes.

In a frying pan over medium-high heat, warm the remaining 1 tablespoon oil. Add the bell peppers and cook, stirring occasionally, until soft, about 10 minutes. Add the vinegar and cook until it evaporates, 1–2 minutes. In a bowl, combine the peppers, eggplant, pine nuts, chopped basil and the 3 cheeses.

Punch down the dough and transfer to a floured work surface. Divide in half. Cover one-half with plastic wrap. Roll out the other half into a round 12 inches (30 cm) in diameter and ¼ inch (6 mm) thick. Transfer to a flour-dusted pizza peel or rimless baking sheet. Spread half of the eggplant mixture over half of the round, leaving a 1-inch (2.5-cm) border. Moisten the border with water, fold the uncovered dough over the filling and seal the edges well.

Slide onto the stone or tiles and bake until golden and crisp, 10–12 minutes. Assemble and bake a second calzone from the remaining ingredients. Garnish with basil sprigs and cut into wedges to serve. *Makes 2 calzones; serves 6*

Chicken Rolled with Pesto

6   **skinless, boneless chicken breast halves, about 6 oz (185 g) each**

    salt and freshly ground pepper

½   **recipe basil pesto** *(recipe on page 16),* **made with ¼ cup (2 fl oz/60 ml) olive oil**

¼   **cup (½ oz/15 g) fresh bread crumbs**

6   **cups (48 fl oz/1.5 l) chicken stock**

1   **tablespoon unsalted butter, at room temperature, cut into pieces**

This dish makes a delicious choice for a picnic because it is equally delicious when served cold or at room temperature. For easy outdoor serving, cut the rolls into slices as directed and omit the sauce. The pesto must be thicker than is customary, so less olive oil is used when making it.

ONE AT A TIME, place the chicken breasts between 2 pieces of waxed paper and, using a meat pounder, pound to an even ¼-inch (6-mm) thickness. Season to taste on both sides with salt and pepper.

Cut out six 8-inch (20-cm) squares of aluminum foil. In a small bowl, combine the pesto and bread crumbs and stir well. Divide the pesto among the chicken breasts, spreading it evenly and leaving a ¼-inch (6-mm) border uncovered. Starting at a short end, roll up each chicken breast, enclosing the stuffing completely. Wrap each chicken roll tightly in a square of the foil and seal the ends closed.

In a frying pan over medium-high heat, bring the chicken stock to a boil. Reduce the heat to medium-low, add the foil rolls and simmer in a single layer, turning occasionally, until slightly firm to the touch, about 20 minutes. Remove the rolls from the stock and set aside.

Increase the heat to high, bring the stock to a boil and boil until reduced to about 1 cup (8 fl oz/250 ml), 10–15 minutes. Remove from the heat and whisk in the butter pieces.

To serve, unwrap the rolls and discard the foil. Cut the rolls on the diagonal into slices ¼ inch (6 mm) thick. Arrange on warmed individual plates and spoon the sauce over the top. Serve immediately. *Serves 6*

Swordfish Steaks with Mango and Avocado Salsa

2   large, ripe mangoes

1   ripe avocado, halved, pitted, peeled and diced

½   fresh jalapeño chili pepper, seeded and minced

⅓   cup (1½ oz/45 g) diced red (Spanish) onion

1   teaspoon grated lime zest

3   tablespoons fresh lime juice

¼   cup (2 fl oz/60 ml) fresh orange juice

¼   cup (⅓ oz/10 g) chopped fresh cilantro (fresh corian-der), plus cilantro sprigs for garnish

2   tablespoons olive oil

    salt and freshly ground pepper

6   swordfish steaks, about 6 oz (185 g) each and 1 inch (2.5 cm) thick

    lime wedges

A nice alternative to traditional tomato salsa, this exotic mix offers an irresistible blend of fruitiness and richness. It is also good with grilled tuna steaks, halibut, snapper or chicken.

WORKING WITH 1 MANGO at a time, cut off the flesh from each side of the big, flat pit, to form 2 large pieces. Discard the pit. Using a knife, score the flesh lengthwise and then crosswise into ½-inch (12-mm) squares, cutting through to the skin. Then, holding the mango over a bowl, slip the blade between the skin and flesh to cut away the flesh, allowing the cubes to fall into a bowl. Add the avocado, jalapeño, onion, lime zest, lime juice, orange juice, chopped cilantro and 1 tablespoon of the olive oil. Mix well and season to taste with salt and pepper. Set aside.

In 1 or 2 frying pans large enough to hold the swordfish steaks in a single layer without crowding, warm the remaining 1 tablespoon olive oil over medium-high heat. Add the swordfish and cook until lightly golden on the first side, about 5 minutes. Turn the fish, season to taste with salt and pepper and continue to cook until lightly golden on the second side and opaque throughout when cut with a knife, about 5 minutes longer.

Place the swordfish steaks on warmed individual plates and top with the salsa. Garnish with lime wedges and cilantro sprigs and serve. *Serves 6*

You must sit down, says Love, and taste my meat: So I did sit and eat.

—George Herbert

Barbecued Pork Ribs

6   **lb (3 kg) pork spareribs, in 2 racks**

     salt and freshly ground black pepper

     barbecue sauce *(recipe on page 17)*

¼   **teaspoon cayenne pepper**

¼   **cup (3 oz/90 g) honey**

Grilling over mesquite imparts a smoky flavor to meats. Watch the ribs closely, turning to brown them evenly and removing them as soon as they are ready. For a smokier flavor, the grill is partially covered during cooking. Serve with corn on the cob and coleslaw for a traditional summer barbecue.

PREHEAT AN OVEN to 350°F (180°C).

Arrange the spareribs in a single layer on a baking sheet. Season on all sides with salt and black pepper. Cover with aluminum foil and bake until tender, 1¼–1½ hours.

Prepare a fire in a charcoal grill.

While the coals are heating, prepare the barbecue sauce, adding the cayenne pepper with the allspice and substituting the honey for the brown sugar.

Remove the ribs from the oven and discard the foil. Place the ribs on the grill rack about 5 inches (13 cm) from the fire and brush with half of the barbecue sauce. Partially cover the grill and cook the ribs for 5–10 minutes. Turn the ribs and baste them with additional sauce. Re-cover the grill partially and continue to cook until golden brown, 5–10 minutes longer.

Transfer the ribs to a cutting board and cut between the ribs into individual pieces. Serve immediately. *Serves 6*

Grilled Leg of Lamb with Lavender-Rosemary Rub

1	leg of lamb, 5–6 lb (2.5–3 kg), boned, trimmed of excess fat and butterflied
3	cloves garlic, thinly sliced
¼	cup (¼ oz/7 g) dried or fresh lavender flowers
3	tablespoons chopped fresh rosemary
3	tablespoons extra-virgin olive oil
	salt and freshly ground pepper
	fresh lavender sprigs or fresh rosemary sprigs

During the summer months, a lovely violet carpet of lavender spreads across the parched hillsides of southern France. The flowers of this member of the mint family add a distinctive floral fragrance to Provençal dishes. The silver-gray leaves are used to make a tisane or herb tea, or as part of the popular herbes de Provence.

MAKE 20 SMALL INCISIONS at regular intervals in the lamb meat. Tuck a garlic slice into each incision.

In a small bowl, combine the lavender flowers, rosemary and olive oil. Rub the mixture over the lamb. Cover and let stand at room temperature for 2 hours or overnight in the refrigerator.

Preheat a broiler (griller), or prepare a fire in a charcoal grill.

Place the lamb on a broiler pan under the broiler or on an oiled grill rack, each about 4 inches (10 cm) from the heat source. Broil or grill until the first side is browned, about 15 minutes. Turn, season well with salt and pepper, and continue to cook until browned on the second side and an instant-read thermometer inserted into the thickest portion registers 130–135°F (54–57°C) for medium-rare or the meat is pink when cut into with a sharp knife, about 15 minutes longer. Transfer to a cutting board, cover with aluminum foil and let rest for 10 minutes before carving.

Cut the lamb across the grain into thin slices and arrange on a warmed platter. Garnish with lavender or rosemary sprigs and serve immediately.

Serves 6–8

Silver-Baked Salmon with Salsa Verde

1	**whole salmon, 6 lb (3 kg), cleaned**
1	**tablespoon kosher salt**
¼	**teaspoon ground pepper**
½	**lemon, thinly sliced, plus lemon wedges for garnish**
4	**fresh parsley sprigs**
4	**fresh thyme sprigs**
4	**fresh oregano sprigs**
2	**tablespoons extra-virgin olive oil**

For the salsa verde:

1	**cup (2 oz/60 g) chopped fresh flat-leaf (Italian) parsley**
½	**cup (1 oz/30 g) chopped fresh chives**
2	**teaspoons chopped fresh oregano**
1	**teaspoon chopped fresh thyme**
½	**teaspoon chopped fresh rosemary**
¼	**cup (2 oz/60 g) drained capers, chopped**
4	**cloves garlic, minced**
¾	**cup (6 fl oz/180 ml) extra-virgin olive oil**
½	**cup (4 fl oz/125 ml) fresh lemon juice**
	salt and ground pepper

This method provides a wonderful and easy way to bake whole salmon and works equally well with a 4-pound (2-kg) center-cut fillet. You may choose to remove the head and tail from the fish before baking, or leave them intact for a more traditional presentation. Garnish with fresh herb sprigs and serve warm, at room temperature or chilled. Grilled Yukon Gold potatoes *(recipe on page 99)* make a nice accompaniment.

PREHEAT AN OVEN to 375°F (190°C).

Rinse the fish and pat dry with paper towels. Rub the cavity and the outside of the fish with the kosher salt and pepper. On a baking sheet large enough to hold the fish flat, lay an 18-inch (45-cm) square of heavy-duty aluminum foil. Place the fish in the center of the foil. Stuff the cavity with the lemon slices and herb sprigs. Close the cavity and rub the outside surface with the olive oil. Cover with a piece of foil of the same size and fold and crimp the edges to make an airtight package.

Bake until the fish flakes easily with a fork or an instant-read thermometer inserted into the thickest part of the fish registers 140°F (60°C), 50–60 minutes.

Meanwhile, make the salsa: In a bowl, mix together the parsley, chives, oregano, thyme, rosemary, capers, garlic, olive oil, lemon juice and salt and pepper to taste. Set aside.

Remove the salmon from the oven. Cut off a corner of the foil package and pour ½ cup (4 fl oz/125 ml) liquid from the package into a frying pan. Crimp the corner closed again to retain the juices. Place the pan over high heat and boil until only 2 tablespoons liquid remain, 1–2 minutes. Remove from the heat and let cool for 5 minutes. Add to the salsa mixture. Mix well.

To serve, place the foil package on a platter and cut open the top. Garnish with lemon wedges. Serve the salsa on the side. *Serves 6–8*

Grilled Fontina and Eggplant Caviar Sandwich

2   **large eggplants (aubergines), 2½ lb (1.25 g) total**

2   **tablespoons fresh lemon juice**

2   **cloves garlic, minced**

1   **teaspoon ground cumin**

½   **teaspoon sweet paprika**

⅛   **teaspoon cayenne pepper**

1   **tablespoon extra-virgin olive oil**

    salt and freshly ground black pepper

2   **tablespoons unsalted butter, at room temperature**

12   **slices coarse-textured white bread**

6   **oz (185 g) Fontina cheese, thinly sliced**

Eggplant caviar is the American version of a Mediterranean eggplant preparation often served as an accompaniment to bread or pita chips, or as a spread for sandwiches. The name *caviar* is derived from the nubby texture of the coarsely chopped mixture.

PREPARE A FIRE in a charcoal grill. Preheat an oven to 400°F (200°C).

When the fire is ready, place the eggplants on an oiled grill rack about 4 inches (10 cm) from the fire and grill, turning occasionally, until soft and black, 10–15 minutes. Transfer the eggplants to a baking sheet and bake until very soft, 15–20 minutes. Remove from the oven and let cool slightly.

Cut the eggplants in half and scoop out the pulp onto a cutting board. Discard the skin. Chop the eggplant coarsely. In a large bowl, combine the eggplant, lemon juice, garlic, cumin, paprika, cayenne pepper and olive oil. Mix well. Season to taste with salt and black pepper.

Place a large frying pan over medium heat. While the pan is heating, spread 1 tablespoon of the butter on one side of 6 bread slices, dividing it evenly, and place them buttered side down on a work surface. Top the slices with half of the Fontina, distributing it evenly, then spread each sandwich with one-sixth of the eggplant mixture. Top with the remaining cheese. Spread the remaining 6 bread slices with the remaining 1 tablespoon butter and place, buttered side up, on the sandwiches.

Place the sandwiches in the hot pan and cook until golden on the first side and the cheese is almost melted, 2–3 minutes. Turn the sandwiches and continue to cook until golden on the second side and the cheese is melted completely, 2–3 minutes longer. Remove from the pan.

Transfer to individual plates and cut in half on the diagonal. Serve immediately. *Serves 6*

Shrimp Kabobs with Lemons and Bay Leaves

36	extra-large shrimp (prawns), about 2 lb (1 kg), peeled and deveined
6	tablespoons (3 fl oz/90 ml) extra-virgin olive oil
24	bay leaves
3	lemons, each cut into 8 wedges
2½	tablespoons fresh lemon juice
1	small clove garlic, minced
1	teaspoon chopped fresh oregano, plus oregano sprigs for garnish
	salt and freshly ground pepper

A great summertime treat, kabobs can be assembled ahead of time and grilled at the last minute. These lemony shrimp-filled skewers are delicious accompanied with steamed couscous or rice.

SOAK 12 BAMBOO SKEWERS, each 8 inches (20 cm) long, in water to cover for 30 minutes.

Prepare a fire in a charcoal grill.

While the coals are heating, place the shrimp in a bowl and add 2 tablespoons of the olive oil. Toss to coat the shrimp evenly. Drain the skewers. Working with 1 skewer at a time, thread a shrimp onto it, piercing each shrimp through the body and again through the tail. Next thread a bay leaf and a lemon wedge diagonally onto the skewer, making sure the skewer pierces the lemon rind. Continue in this manner, ending with a shrimp, until the skewer holds 3 shrimp in all. Repeat with the remaining skewers and ingredients. Set aside until ready to grill.

In a small bowl, whisk together the remaining 4 tablespoons (2 fl oz/60 ml) olive oil, the lemon juice, garlic and chopped oregano and season to taste with salt and pepper to form a vinaigrette. Set aside.

Place the kabobs on an oiled grill rack about 4 inches (10 cm) from the fire. Grill, turning every few minutes, until the shrimp are almost firm to the touch, 5–7 minutes.

Transfer to a warmed platter, drizzle with the vinaigrette and garnish with oregano sprigs. *Serves 6*

Nut-Crusted Trout with Romesco Sauce

For the romesco sauce:

5   tablespoons (3 fl oz/80 ml) extra-virgin olive oil

1   slice coarse-textured white bread

¼   cup (1½ oz/45 g) blanched almonds

1   cup (6 oz/185 g) peeled, seeded and chopped tomatoes *(see technique, page 15)*

1   clove garlic, minced

2   teaspoons sweet paprika

¼   teaspoon red pepper flakes

3   tablespoons red wine vinegar

    salt and freshly ground pepper

For the trout:

2   cups (11 oz/345 g) plain almonds (skins intact)

½   cup (2½ oz/75 g) all-purpose (plain) flour

3   eggs

    salt and freshly ground pepper

6   whole trout, 10 oz (315 g) each, cleaned

1   tablespoon unsalted butter

1   tablespoon olive oil

Trout season begins in the spring and runs to early fall. Although nothing can compare to the flavor of a fish you have reeled in yourself, most markets stock a variety of hatchery-bred trout that work equally well in this recipe.

TO MAKE THE SAUCE, in a frying pan over medium heat, warm 1 tablespoon of the olive oil. Add the bread and fry, turning occasionally, until golden on both sides, 2–3 minutes. Transfer the bread to a food processor fitted with the metal blade. Add the blanched almonds to the same frying pan and cook over medium heat, stirring often, until golden, about 2 minutes. Remove from the heat and transfer to the processor. Add the tomatoes, garlic, paprika and red pepper flakes to the processor and process until a rough paste forms, about 1 minute. With the motor running, pour in the vinegar and the remaining 4 tablespoons (2 fl oz/60 ml) olive oil in a slow, steady stream and process until barely fluid, about 1 minute longer. Season to taste with salt and pepper. Pour into a bowl and let stand at room temperature for 1 hour before using.

To prepare the trout, rinse the processor bowl and refit it with the metal blade. Add the plain almonds and process to chop finely. Transfer to a shallow bowl. Place the flour and eggs in separate shallow bowls. Whisk the eggs until blended and season to taste with salt and pepper. Season the flour as well. One at a time, dip the trout into the flour, patting off the excess, then into the egg and then lightly into the almonds. Set aside on a platter.

In a large, heavy frying pan over medium heat, melt the butter with the oil. Add the trout and cook until lightly golden on the first side, 4–5 minutes. Turn and continue to cook until golden on the second side and cooked through, 4–5 minutes longer.

Serve the trout on individual plates with the sauce alongside. *Serves 6*

Tuna Burgers with Ginger-Mustard Mayonnaise

⅓ cup (3 fl oz/80 ml) mayonnaise

2 teaspoons fresh lemon juice

1 teaspoon Asian sesame oil

1½ teaspoons peeled and grated fresh ginger

1 tablespoon whole-grain mustard

1 clove garlic, minced

salt and freshly ground pepper

6 good-quality hamburger rolls, split

2 lb (1 kg) tuna fillets, about ¾ inch (2 cm) thick, cut into 6 equal pieces

olive oil

6 large lettuce leaves

6 thin slices red onion

Fresh tuna fillets offer a healthful alternative to hamburgers. This classy grilled sandwich can also be made with swordfish, grouper, snapper or salmon. Slices of tomato or avocado can be added along with the lettuce.

PREPARE A FIRE in a charcoal grill.

In a small bowl, whisk together the mayonnaise, lemon juice, sesame oil, ginger, mustard, garlic and salt and pepper to taste. Set aside.

Lightly brush the cut sides of the rolls with the mayonnaise mixture. Lightly oil the grill rack. Place the rolls, cut sides down, on the grill rack about 4 inches (10 cm) from the fire and grill until lightly golden. Set the rolls around the perimeter of the grill rack, away from the coals, to keep warm. Lightly brush the tuna with olive oil and place on the grill rack. Grill until golden on the first side, about 4 minutes. Turn, season to taste with salt and pepper, and continue to cook until golden on the second side but still slightly pink at the center, 3–4 minutes longer, or until done to your liking.

Remove from the grill, placing each piece of tuna on the bottom half of a roll. Top each with an equal amount of the mayonnaise mixture, a lettuce leaf and an onion slice and the other half of the roll. Serve immediately. *Serves 6*

side dishes

Orzo-and-Feta-Stuffed Tomatoes

1¼ cups (8½ oz/265 g) dried orzo

1 tablespoon extra-virgin olive oil

ice water as needed

6 ripe but firm tomatoes, any color

6 oz (185 g) feta cheese, crumbled

½ cup (2½ oz/75 g) finely diced English (hothouse) cucumber

½ cup (2½ oz/75 g) finely diced red (Spanish) onion

1½ tablespoons fresh lemon juice

3 tablespoons chopped fresh dill

3 tablespoons chopped fresh mint

salt and freshly ground pepper

Stuffed tomatoes are a wonderful partner to grilled meats, and can also be served alone as a first course or even a light main course for an al fresco lunch. Rice-shaped orzo pasta is delicious partnered with other filling ingredients. For example, mix the same amount of orzo with 1 cup (6 oz/ 185 g) fresh-cooked crab or lobster meat; 1 cup (6 oz/185 g) corn kernels, blanched for 1 minute and drained; and ¼ cup (¾ oz/20 g) thinly sliced green (spring) onion.

BRING A LARGE SAUCEPAN three-fourths full of salted water to a rolling boil over high heat. Add the orzo and cook until al dente (tender but firm to the bite), 5–8 minutes or according to the package directions. Drain and place in a bowl. Immediately add the olive oil and toss well. Cover and refrigerate until well chilled, at least 1 hour or for up to 24 hours.

Meanwhile, have ready a large bowl of ice water. Bring another large saucepan three-fourths full of water to a boil. Add the tomatoes and blanch for no more than 15 seconds. Using a slotted spoon, transfer to the ice water to cool completely. Cut a slice ¾ inch (2 cm) thick off the stem end of each tomato and set aside. Using a spoon, carefully scoop out the pulp, leaving sturdy shells; discard the pulp or reserve for another use. Place, cut sides down, on paper towels to drain until ready to use.

In a large bowl, mix together the chilled orzo, feta, cucumber, onion, lemon juice, dill and mint. Season to taste with salt and pepper.

Place each tomato, cut side up, on a serving plate. Spoon the orzo and feta mixture into the tomatoes, distributing it evenly. Place the tomato tops over the filling, cover and chill for 30 minutes.

Place the tomatoes on individual plates and serve. *Serves 6*

...rich chocolate earth studded emerald green, frothed with the white of cauliflowers, jewelled with the purple globes of eggplant and the scarlet wealth of tomatoes.

—Doris Lessing

Grilled Vegetable Ratatouille

olive oil for the grill rack, plus 2 tablespoons olive oil

2   eggplants (aubergines), 1 lb (500 g) each, cut crosswise into slices 1 inch (2.5 cm) thick

4   small zucchini (courgettes), ¾ lb (375 g) total, cut crosswise into slices 1 inch (2.5 cm) thick

2   yellow onions, cut into slices 1 inch (2.5 cm) thick

3   red, yellow, orange or green bell peppers (capsicums), or a mixture

5   tomatoes, 1–1¼ lb (500–625 g) total

4   cloves garlic, minced

¼   cup (⅓ oz/10 g) chopped fresh flat-leaf (Italian) parsley

½   teaspoon chopped fresh thyme

2   tablespoons red wine vinegar

salt and freshly ground pepper

20 fresh basil leaves, cut into thin strips

Throughout Provence, there are many versions of this thick vegetable ragout. In this recipe, the vegetables are first grilled separately and then stewed together. Ratatouille often tastes even better the next day, so you may wish to make it a day in advance, then reheat it on the stove top before serving. If you have leftover ratatouille, pair it with sliced grilled chicken in a sandwich.

PREPARE A FIRE in a charcoal grill.

When the fire is ready, brush the grill liberally with olive oil. Place the eggplant, zucchini and onion slices, the bell peppers and the tomatoes on the grill rack about 4 inches (10 cm) from the fire. Grill, turning frequently, until lightly golden, about 5 minutes. As the vegetables are ready, remove all of them, except the bell peppers; keep the vegetables separate. Continue to cook the bell peppers until the skin is blackened and blistered, then remove from the grill, cover with aluminum foil and let steam until cool enough to handle, about 10 minutes. Peel off the skins and cut the peppers in half lengthwise. Remove the stems, seeds and ribs and cut the peppers into strips. Cut the egg-plant and onion slices and the whole tomatoes into 1-inch (2.5-cm) dice. Keep all of the vegetables separate.

In a large, heavy pot over medium heat, warm the 2 tablespoons olive oil. Add the onions and cook, stirring, until soft, about 7 minutes. Add the eggplant, bell peppers, zucchini, and tomatoes and cook uncovered, stirring occasionally, until all the vegetables are tender, 30–40 minutes. Add the garlic, parsley, thyme and vinegar, stir well and cook for 5 minutes longer to blend the flavors. Season to taste with salt and pepper. Transfer to a platter and garnish with the basil. Serve warm or at room temperature. *Serves 6*

Green and Yellow Beans with Summer Savory

1   **lb (500 g) green beans, trimmed**

1   **lb (500 g) yellow beans, trimmed**

1   **fresh poblano chili pepper**

1   **teaspoon unsalted butter**

1   **teaspoon olive oil**

2   **tablespoons chopped fresh summer savory, plus summer savory sprigs for garnish**

      salt and freshly ground pepper

Few herbs complement fresh snap beans better than summer savory. With a flavor resembling a cross between mint and thyme and masked with a slightly peppery taste, savory's assertiveness offers an ideal foil for the beans' sun-ripened mellowness and the chili's mild heat.

BRING A LARGE SAUCEPAN three-fourths full of salted water to a boil over medium-high heat. Add the green and yellow beans and cook until tender, 4–6 minutes. Drain and rinse under cold running water to halt the cooking. Set aside.

Preheat a broiler (griller). Cut the chili pepper in half lengthwise and remove the stem, seeds and ribs. Place the pepper halves, cut sides down, on a baking sheet. Broil (grill) until the skins are blackened and blistered. Remove from the broiler and cover loosely with aluminum foil. Let steam until cool enough to handle, about 10 minutes, then peel off the skin. Cut the pepper halves lengthwise into strips about ¼ inch (6 mm) wide.

In a large frying pan over medium heat, melt the butter with the olive oil. Add the beans, chili pepper strips and chopped savory and cook, stirring frequently, until hot, about 2 minutes. Season to taste with salt and pepper.

Transfer to a warmed platter and garnish with savory sprigs. Serve immediately. *Serves 6*

I myself am quite absorbed by the...delicate yellow, delicate soft green, delicate violet of a ploughed and weeded piece of soil, regularly chequered by the green of flowering potato-plants...

—Vincent van Gogh

Grilled Yukon Gold Potatoes with Garlic and Herbs

2½ lb (1.25 kg) small Yukon Gold potatoes

3 heads garlic

2 tablespoons extra-virgin olive oil

salt and freshly ground pepper

15 fresh thyme sprigs, coarsely chopped

6 fresh rosemary sprigs, coarsely chopped

Yukon Golds are yellow-gold potatoes with an assertive flavor and a creamy texture. Whole cloves of garlic, scattered over the potatoes in the roasting pan, add to their memorable flavor. For those who like extra garlic taste, the browned sheaths can be removed and the whole garlic cloves enjoyed with the grilled potatoes. This recipe is a great one for preparing in advance: roast the potatoes up to 2 days ahead, and then throw them onto the grill at the last minute to warm them up.

PREHEAT AN OVEN to 375°F (190°C).

Rinse the potatoes but do not dry them. Cut them in half and place in a 9-by-13-inch (23-by-33-cm) baking dish. Remove the outer papery sheaths from the garlic heads. Cut each garlic head in half through the stem end. Break up the garlic and sprinkle the cloves over the potatoes. Drizzle with the olive oil and season to taste with salt and pepper. Toss the potatoes so they are completely coated with the oil. Sprinkle the thyme and rosemary over the potatoes.

Cover tightly with aluminum foil. Bake until the potatoes are tender when pierced with a knife, about 1 hour.

Meanwhile, prepare a fire in a charcoal grill.

Remove the potatoes from the pan and place on the grill rack about 4 inches (10 cm) from the fire; reserve the garlic cloves in the pan until ready to serve. Grill the potatoes until golden on the first side, 3–4 minutes. Turn and continue to grill until golden on the second side and hot throughout, 3–4 minutes longer.

Transfer the potatoes to a platter and sprinkle the reserved garlic cloves over the top. Serve immediately. *Serves 6*

The trouble is, you cannot grow just one zucchini…
At night, you will be able to hear the ground quake as
more and more zucchinis erupt.

—Dave Barry

Summer Squash Sauté

5	small zucchini (courgettes), 1 lb (500 g) total
4	small yellow summer or crookneck squashes, 1 lb (500 g) total
4	pattypan (custard) squashes, ¾ lb (375 g) total
2	tablespoons extra-virgin olive oil
2	cloves garlic, minced
2	tablespoons chopped fresh basil
1	teaspoon chopped fresh oregano
½	teaspoon chopped fresh marjoram
	salt and freshly ground pepper
	zucchini (courgette) blossoms, optional
	fresh herb sprigs, optional

Squashes, members of the gourd family, are native to the Western Hemisphere. There are two basic types of squash, summer and winter. Summer varieties have thin, edible skin, tender seeds and a high water content, while winter squashes have tough, hard skin and seeds.

CUT THE ZUCCHINI and the summer or crookneck squashes crosswise into rounds ½ inch (12 mm) thick. Cut the pattypan squash in half horizontally and then crosswise into pieces ½ inch (12 mm) thick.

In a frying pan over medium-high heat, warm the olive oil. Add all of the squashes and cook, stirring occasionally, until tender when pierced with a fork, 10–12 minutes. Stir in the garlic, basil, oregano and marjoram. Season to taste with salt and pepper.

To serve, place the squash in a serving bowl and garnish with squash blossoms and herb sprigs, if desired. *Serves 6*

And at noon he would come
Up from the garden, his hard crooked hands
Gentle with earth, his knees earth-stained, smelling
Of sun, of summer…

—Archibald MacLeish

Grilled "Thick-Slice" Red Onions

6   **large red (Spanish) onions, cut into slices ¾ inch (2 cm) thick**

1   **tablespoon olive oil**

3   **tablespoons extra-virgin olive oil**

1½ **tablespoons balsamic vinegar**

1   **teaspoon chopped fresh summer savory, thyme or oregano, plus summer savory, thyme or oregano sprigs for garnish**

   salt and freshly ground pepper

Red onions are a particularly mild onion variety and grilling only heightens their natural sweetness. These smoky slices pair well with lamb, fish, chicken or beef. They can also be served as a first course with plenty of crusty bread to soak up the juices. Any leftovers can be slipped into a grilled steak sandwich.

PREPARE A FIRE in a charcoal grill.

While the coals are heating, brush each onion slice on both sides with the olive oil.

In a small bowl, whisk together the extra-virgin olive oil, vinegar, chopped herb and salt and pepper to taste to form a vinaigrette.

Place the onions on the grill rack about 5 inches (13 cm) from the fire. Grill until golden on the first side, 5–6 minutes. Carefully turn the onions and continue to grill until tender and golden on the second side, 5–6 minutes longer.

Transfer to a warmed platter, drizzle with the vinaigrette and garnish with herb sprigs. *Serves 6*

The corn is as high as an elephant's eye,
An' it looks like it's climbin' clear up to the sky.

—Oscar Hammerstein II

6	ears of corn with husks intact
½	teaspoon salt
¼	teaspoon freshly ground black pepper
1	teaspoon chili powder
½	teaspoon ground cumin
⅛	teaspoon cayenne pepper
2	tablespoons unsalted butter, melted

Chili-Rubbed Corn on the Cob

Corn on the cob celebrates the very soul of summer. Some purists will go so far as to eat corn only if it was picked less than half a dozen hours before serving. To test for freshness, stick the nail of your index finger into a kernel. If the center of the kernel shoots into the air, the corn is truly fresh.

PULL BACK THE HUSKS from each ear of corn but leave them attached to the base of the cob. Pull off and discard the silks. Rinse the ears under running water and then place in a sink with cold water to cover. Let soak for 20 minutes to saturate the corn husks and add moisture to the kernels.

Meanwhile, prepare a fire in a charcoal grill.

In a small bowl, stir together the salt, black pepper, chili powder, cumin, cayenne pepper and butter. Brush the ears of corn with the butter mixture and rewrap the husks around them. Wrap each ear of corn in aluminum foil.

Place the corn on a grill rack about 4 inches (10 cm) from the fire. Grill, turning occasionally, until the corn is tender, about 15 minutes. To test, open a package; the corn kernels should be tender when pierced with a fork.

Remove the foil and arrange the corn cobs on a warmed platter. Serve immediately. *Serves 6*

desserts

Latticed Cherry Pie

The first cherries arrive in late spring and are available into the early summer.

For the pastry:

2   cups (10 oz/315 g) all-purpose (plain) flour, plus flour as needed

½   teaspoon salt

7   tablespoons (3½ oz/105 g) unsalted butter, chilled, cut into pieces

½   cup (4 oz/125 g) vegetable shortening, chilled, cut into pieces

3   tablespoons ice water

1   teaspoon cider vinegar

For the filling:

1¾ lb (875 g) sweet cherries such as Royal Ann, Bing or Rainier, pitted

¾   cup (6 oz/185 g) sugar

2   tablespoons all-purpose (plain) flour

1   teaspoon kirsch or quetsch (plum liqueur)

1   egg yolk

1   tablespoon milk

    vanilla ice cream

To make the dough, in a bowl, stir together the flour and salt. Using a pastry blender or 2 knives, cut in the butter and shortening until the mixture resembles coarse meal. In a cup or small bowl, combine the water and vinegar. Sprinkle the mixture over the top and, using a fork, toss lightly to moisten evenly. Gather the dough into a ball, being careful not to work it too much, and place on a lightly floured work surface. Divide the dough in half and wrap each half in plastic wrap. Chill for at least 4 hours or for up to 24 hours.

Using a rolling pin, roll out 1 ball of dough on a lightly floured work surface into a round 12 inches (30 cm) in diameter and ⅛ inch (3 mm) thick. Fold the dough in half and then into quarters and transfer it to a 9-inch (23-cm) pie pan. Unfold and gently press into the pan. Trim the edges flush with the pan rim. Place in the freezer for 30 minutes.

Position a rack in the lower part of an oven and preheat to 400°F (200°C). Meanwhile, to make the filling, toss together the cherries, sugar, flour and liqueur.

Remove the remaining dough from the refrigerator and roll out into a round about 11 inches (28 cm) in diameter. Using a small knife or a pastry wheel, cut into strips about ¾ inch (2 cm) wide. Place a large sheet of waxed paper on the work surface and dust lightly with flour. Placing the strips about ¼ inch (6 mm) apart, weave them on the waxed paper to form a lattice.

Remove the pastry shell from the freezer and turn the cherry mixture into it. Gently lift the waxed paper over the filling and carefully slide the lattice onto the pie. Trim the edges flush with the pan rim and crimp to form an attractive edge. In a small bowl, beat together the egg yolk and milk and brush over the lattice and pastry edge.

Bake until the juices bubble thickly and the crust is golden, 1–1¼ hours. Transfer to a rack to cool for 1 hour before serving. Accompany each slice with a scoop of ice cream. *Makes one 9-inch (23-cm) pie; serves 6–8*

The odors of fruits waft me to my southern home,
to my childhood frolics in the peach orchard.

—Helen Keller

Peach Ice Cream with Rose Petals

For the rose petals:

1   cup (1½ oz/45 g) very loosely packed pesticide-free rose petals, in any color

2   egg whites

2   tablespoons water

1   cup (7 oz/220 g) superfine (caster) sugar

For the ice cream:

6   egg yolks

¾   cup (6 oz/185 g) granulated sugar

1   cup (8 fl oz/250 ml) milk

2   cups (16 fl oz/500 ml) heavy (double) cream

     few drops vanilla extract (essence)

5   very ripe, flavorful peaches *(see note)*, 1¼ lb (625 g) total, blanched in boiling water for 1 minute, drained, peeled, halved and pitted

Freestone peaches are well suited to ice cream making. Use either the O'Henry, Elberta, First Lady or the floral-scented white Babcock variety here.

TO PREPARE THE ROSE PETALS, rinse gently and place on paper towels until completely dry. In a bowl, combine the egg whites and water and whisk lightly to break up the whites. Line a baking sheet with waxed paper or parchment paper. Using tweezers to hold a petal by its base, brush the egg wash on both sides. Then, holding the petal over the prepared baking sheet, sprinkle with the superfine sugar. Continue with the remaining petals, placing them in a single layer on the baking sheet. Let stand uncovered at room temperature, turning the petals occasionally, until dry and crisp, 2–4 days, depending upon the temperature and humidity.

To make the ice cream, in a saucepan, whisk together the egg yolks and ½ cup (4 oz/125 g) of the sugar until well mixed. In another saucepan, combine the milk and cream over medium heat and heat until small bubbles form along the edges of the pan. Remove from the heat and very gradually add the cream mixture to the yolk mixture, whisking constantly. Place over medium heat and heat, stirring constantly, until the mixture begins to thicken and coats the back of a wooden spoon, or until an instant-read thermometer inserted into the liquid registers 165°F (74°C), about 5 minutes. Remove from the heat and strain through a fine-mesh sieve into a bowl. Add the vanilla and whisk to cool the mixture for 1 minute, then cover and chill well, about 2 hours.

Place the peach halves in a bowl. Add the remaining ¼ cup (2 oz/60 g) sugar and, using a potato masher, mash until you have a mixture with tiny pieces of peach. Strain through a coarse-mesh sieve into another bowl. Let stand for 15 minutes, then stir into the chilled ice cream base.

Freeze in an ice cream maker according to the manufacturer's directions. Scoop the ice cream into chilled bowls and garnish with the rose petals.
Makes about 1½ qt (1.5 l); serves 6–8

I know I am but summer to your heart,
And not the full four seasons of the year.

—Edna St. Vincent Millay

Summer Berry Gratin

5   **egg yolks**

1   **teaspoon cornstarch (cornflour)**

⅓   **cup (3 oz/90 g) granulated sugar**

2   **tablespoons all-purpose (plain) flour**

1½   **cups (12 fl oz/375 ml) milk**

½   **teaspoon vanilla extract (essence)**

1   **tablespoon kirsch, framboise or crème de cassis**

1   **tablespoon unsalted butter, at room temperature**

½   **cup (4 fl oz/125 ml) mascarpone cheese**

4   **cups (1 lb/500 g) mixed berries such as blueberries, blackberries, raspberries and boysenberries, in any combination**

1   **tablespoon confectioners' (icing) sugar**

All kinds of summer berries or fruits can be used for this versatile dessert. Try peaches, nectarines or plums in place of the mixed berries used here. You can make the pastry cream and ready the berries several hours in advance. When it is time to serve the dessert, just assemble and broil.

IN A BOWL, using a whisk or an electric mixer, beat the egg yolks until light and fluffy, 1–2 minutes. In another bowl, stir together the cornstarch, granulated sugar and flour. Add the flour mixture to the egg yolks and again beat until light and fluffy, about 1 minute.

Pour the milk into a saucepan over medium heat and heat until small bubbles appear along the edges of the pan. Gradually add the milk to the egg mixture, whisking constantly. Pour the mixture back into the saucepan and place over low heat. Cook, stirring, until the mixture thickens and bubbles around the edges, 2–3 minutes. Remove from the heat and whisk in the vanilla, liqueur and butter. Fold in the mascarpone.

Preheat a broiler (griller). Divide the custard mixture evenly among 6 flameproof 4-inch (10-cm) gratin or tartlet dishes. Gently press the berries into the custard mixture, dividing them evenly. Sprinkle the tops evenly with the confectioners' sugar. Slip under the broiler about 4 inches (10 cm) from the heat source and broil (grill) until the tops are golden brown, 1–2 minutes. Serve immediately. *Serves 6*

Thy morning bounties ere I left my home,
The biscuit, or confectionary plum.

—William Cowper

Mixed Plum Shortcake

There are more varieties of plums than any other stone fruit. The common Santa Rosa has red skin and tart yellow flesh, while the El Dorado is large, heart shaped and almost black. The Laroda has reddish yellow skin and sweet, firm yellow flesh, and the Kelsey is dark green, turning yellow when ripe.

PREHEAT AN OVEN to 400°F (200°C).

To make the shortcakes, sift together the flour, salt and baking powder into a bowl. Add the butter and, using your fingertips, rub it in until the mixture resembles coarse meal. Using a fork, gradually stir in the buttermilk until the mixture holds together. Gather the dough into a ball and transfer to a well-floured work surface. Using a floured rolling pin, roll out into a round ½ inch (12 mm) thick. Fold in half and roll out again ½ inch (12 mm) thick. Repeat once more. Using a round biscuit cutter 2½–3 inches (6–7.5 cm) in diameter, cut out 6 rounds. Reroll the scraps and cut out 2 additional rounds. Place on an ungreased baking sheet, spacing them well apart. Bake until the tops are lightly golden, about 10 minutes. Transfer to a rack to cool.

To make the filling, halve and pit ¾ lb (375 g) of the plums and place in a blender. Process on high speed until smooth. Strain through a fine-mesh sieve into a large bowl. In a small saucepan over high heat, combine the water and granulated sugar and stir until slightly thickened, about 30 seconds. Add the sugar syrup and liqueur to the plum purée. Halve and pit the remaining 2 lb (1 kg) plums and cut into ½-inch (12-mm) wedges. Toss well with the purée.

To prepare the whipped cream, using a whisk or an electric mixer, beat the cream just until it begins to thicken. Add the liqueur and confectioners' sugar and continue to beat until soft peaks form.

To serve, cut each shortcake in half horizontally. Place the bottoms on individual plates, cut sides up. Spoon the plum mixture and the cream over them. Crown with the tops, cut sides down. Using a sieve or sifter, dust the tops with the confectioners' sugar. Serve immediately. *Serves 6–8*

For the shortcakes:

2½ cups (12½ oz/390 g) all-purpose (plain) flour

¼ teaspoon salt

1 tablespoon baking powder

½ cup (4 oz/125 g) unsalted butter, at room temperature, cut into pieces

1 cup (8 fl oz/250 ml) buttermilk, at room temperature

For the filling:

2¾ lb (1.4 kg) assortment of any 3 plum varieties *(see note)*

⅔ cup (5 fl oz/160 ml) water

¼ cup (2 oz/60 g) granulated sugar

1½ tablespoons quetsch (plum liqueur) or kirsch

For the whipped cream:

1 cup (8 fl oz/250 ml) heavy (double) cream

1 teaspoon quetsch (plum liqueur) or kirsch

1 tablespoon confectioners' (icing) sugar

2 tablespoons confectioners' (icing) sugar for dusting

Fresh Fruit Tart

For the pastry:

1   **cup (5 oz/155 g) all-purpose (plain) flour**

1   **tablespoon sugar**

¼   **teaspoon salt**

½   **cup (4 oz/125 g) unsalted butter, out of the refrigerator for 20 minutes, cut into pieces**

1–2 **tablespoons water**

For the filling:

1¼ **cups (10 fl oz/310 ml) milk**

3½ **tablespoons all-purpose (plain) flour**

¼   **cup (2 oz/60 g) sugar**

4   **egg yolks**

1   **tablespoon unsalted butter**

2   **teaspoons kirsch or ½ teaspoon vanilla extract (essence)**

4   **cups (about 1½ lb/750 g) sliced mixed fruits such as kiwifruits, peaches, plums and whole blueberries**

¼   **cup (2½ oz/75 g) red currant jelly, melted**

TO MAKE THE PASTRY, in a food processor fitted with the metal blade, combine the flour, sugar and salt. Pulse briefly to mix. Add the butter and process until the consistency of coarse meal. With the motor running, add just enough of the water to form a ball that cleans the sides of the bowl. Remove from the processor, wrap the dough in plastic wrap and chill for 30 minutes.

Place the pastry in a 9-inch (23-cm) tart pan with a removable bottom and press it gently onto the bottom and sides of the pan, forming an even layer. Place in the freezer for 30 minutes. Preheat an oven to 375°F (190°C).

Line the pastry shell with parchment paper and fill with pie weights, rice or beans. Bake until lightly golden around the edges, 15–20 minutes. Remove from the oven and remove the weights and parchment. Continue to bake until pale gold, 5–7 minutes. Let cool on a rack.

To make the filling, first make the pastry cream: Pour the milk into a saucepan over medium heat and heat until small bubbles appear along the edges of the pan. Remove from the heat. In another saucepan, stir together the flour and sugar. In a bowl, whisk the egg yolks until light colored. Whisk the hot milk into the flour mixture and place over medium heat. Cook, stirring constantly, until the mixture boils, 1–2 minutes. Remove from the heat and whisk one-fourth of the hot mixture into the egg yolks. Then whisk the egg yolks into the remaining hot mixture and cook over medium heat, stirring constantly, until thickened slightly and an instant-read thermometer inserted into the liquid registers 165°F (74°C), 2–3 minutes. Remove from the heat, stir in the butter and strain through a fine-mesh sieve into a clean bowl. Stir in the kirsch or vanilla and cover with plastic wrap, pressing it directly onto the surface of the pastry cream. Let cool in the refrigerator.

Spread the cooled pastry cream in the pastry shell. Arrange the fruits attractively on top of the pastry cream and brush the fruit with a thin coating of the jelly. Remove the pan sides and, using a spatula, slide the tart from the pan bottom onto a serving plate. *Makes one 9-inch (23-cm) tart; serves 8*

Watermelon Granita

4–5 packed cups (1½ lb/750 g) seedless watermelon chunks

1 cup (8 fl oz/250 ml) water

1 cup (8 oz/250 g) sugar

1 tablespoon fresh lemon juice

Granita is a cooling, icy slush made during the furnacelike summers of Italy. Like ice cream, granitas come in a variety of sweet, refreshing flavors, such as melon, peach, nectarine, berry or coffee. If you like, garnish this granita with tiny wedges of well-chilled watermelon.

PLACE THE WATERMELON CHUNKS in a blender and purée until smooth. Strain through a fine-mesh sieve into a bowl. You should have 2 cups (16 fl oz/500 ml) purée.

In a saucepan over high heat, combine the water and sugar. Heat, stirring, just until the sugar dissolves. Add the sugar syrup and lemon juice to the watermelon purée and stir well. Pour the mixture into a shallow 9-by-13-inch (23-by-33-cm) metal or glass baking dish.

Place, uncovered, in the freezer until ice crystals begin to form, 1½–2 hours. Using a fork, stir to break up the mixture. Return to the freezer and freeze, stirring with the fork every 30 minutes to prevent the mixture from forming a solid mass. It should be evenly crystallized and like slush in another 2 hours.

To serve, spoon or scoop the granita into chilled serving dishes. *Serves 6*

Blueberry Sorbet with Berry and Cassis Compote

For the compote:

2	cups (8 oz/250 g) raspberries
½	cup (4 fl oz/125 ml) water
⅓	cup (2½ oz/75 g) sugar
1	piece lemon peel, about 2 inches (5 cm) long
¾	cup (3 oz/90 g) blueberries
¾	cup (3 oz/90 g) fraises des bois *(see note)*
1	tablespoon crème de cassis
1	teaspoon fresh lemon juice

For the sorbet:

6	cups (1½ lb/750 g) blueberries
1	cup (8 oz/250 g) sugar
½	teaspoon fresh lemon juice

Fraises des bois, tiny wild strawberries from the French Alps, have the scent and flavor of roses. They are easy to grow and do well as an ornamental in any spring or summer garden with part shade and part sunshine. But use them quickly after picking, for they are quite fragile. If fraises des bois are unavailable, double the amount of blueberries in the compote.

TO MAKE THE COMPOTE, place 1 cup (4 oz/125 g) of the raspberries in a food processor fitted with the metal blade or in a blender and purée until smooth. Strain through a fine-mesh sieve into a clean bowl.

In a saucepan over medium-high heat, combine the water, sugar and lemon peel and bring to a boil. Reduce the heat to medium and add the blueberries. Cook until the blueberries just begin to crack, about 1 minute. Remove from the heat and remove the lemon peel and discard. Stir in the fraises des bois, raspberry purée, crème de cassis, lemon juice and the remaining 1 cup (4 oz/125 g) raspberries. Cover and chill for at least 30 minutes.

To make the sorbet, place the blueberries in a food processor fitted with the metal blade or in a blender and purée until smooth. Strain through a fine-mesh sieve into a clean bowl. You should have 2 cups (16 fl oz/500 ml) blueberry purée. Place approximately one-fourth of the purée in a small saucepan over medium heat. Add the sugar and stir until dissolved. Remove from the heat and stir the hot blueberry mixture into the reserved blueberry purée. Add the lemon juice, cover and chill well, about 2 hours.

Freeze the blueberry purée in an ice cream maker according to the manufacturer's directions.

To serve, scoop the sorbet into chilled bowls. Spoon the compote over the top. *Makes about 1 qt (1 l) sorbet and 2 cups (16 fl oz/500 ml) compote; serves 6–8*

The cucumber is a sort of low comedian in a company where the melon is a minor gentleman.

—Charles Dudley Warner

Summer Melons in Spiced White Wine

2   **cups (16 fl oz/500 ml) late-harvest dessert wine such as Muscat or Sauternes**

1   **tablespoon honey**

4   **slices fresh ginger, each ¼ inch (6 mm) thick**

½   **vanilla bean**

5   **lb (2.5 kg) assorted summer melons such as cantaloupe, honeydew, Crenshaw, Casaba and Persian, in any combination**

This is a light, refreshing finale to a meal served on a balmy evening or at Sunday midday. Peaches, nectarines, plums, blackberries or blueberries can be substituted for the melons. Serve with biscotti on the side, if you like.

IN A SAUCEPAN, combine the wine, honey and ginger. Split the vanilla bean in half lengthwise and scrape the seeds into the pan, then add the pod halves as well. Place over high heat and bring to a boil. Reduce the heat to low and simmer, uncovered, for 5 minutes. Remove from the heat. Discard the vanilla pods and ginger slices and let cool.

Meanwhile, halve the melons. Scoop out the seeds and discard. Using a melon baller, scoop out balls of the melon flesh and place them in a large bowl. Pour the cooled spiced wine over the melon, cover and chill for 1 hour.

To serve, divide the melon evenly among chilled individual bowls, spooning some of the wine over each portion. *Serves 6*

Fig and Raspberry Clafouti

1	lb (500 g) figs, halved through the stem end
1	cup (4 oz/125 g) raspberries
¼	cup (1½ oz/45 g) whole almonds
2	tablespoons all-purpose (plain) flour
¾	cup (6 fl oz/180 ml) milk
6	tablespoons (3 oz/90 g) granulated sugar
2	eggs
1	tablespoon framboise or kirsch
	pinch of salt
2	tablespoons unsalted butter, cut into small pieces
1	cup (8 fl oz/250 ml) heavy (double) cream
2	teaspoons confectioners' (icing) sugar
¼	teaspoon vanilla extract (essence)

Most fig varieties are available from June to October. They are extremely perishable and should be eaten as soon as possible after they are picked or purchased. If you must store them, lay them on a baking sheet lined with a kitchen towel or paper towels, and place them, uncovered, in the refrigerator. Figs are at their best when the skins have cracked slightly.

PREHEAT AN OVEN to 400°F (200°C). Butter a 2-qt (2-l) gratin or other baking dish.

Arrange the figs, cut sides up, in the prepared baking dish. Sprinkle the raspberries around and on top of the figs. Set aside.

In a blender or in a food processor fitted with the metal blade, combine the almonds and flour and process until finely ground. Add the milk, 4 tablespoons (2 oz/60 g) of the granulated sugar, the eggs, framboise or kirsch and salt. Process until well mixed, about 30 seconds. Pour the milk mixture over the fruit. Dot the fruit with the butter pieces and sprinkle the remaining 2 tablespoons granulated sugar over the top.

Bake until the top is golden and the custard is set, 30–35 minutes. Transfer to a rack and let cool for 15 minutes.

While the clafouti is cooling, pour the cream into a bowl. Using a whisk or an electric mixer, beat the cream just until it begins to thicken. Add the confectioners' sugar and vanilla and continue to beat until soft peaks form.

Spoon the warm clafouti onto individual plates and pass the cream at the table. *Serves 6*

The blushing apricot and woolly peach
Hang on thy walls, that every child may reach.

—Ben Johnson

Apricot and Blackberry Cobbler

For the topping:

1½ cups (7½ oz/235 g) all-purpose (plain) flour, plus flour as needed

2 tablespoons granulated sugar

2½ teaspoons baking powder

¼ teaspoon salt

6 tablespoons (3 oz/90 g) unsalted butter, cut into pieces

6–8 tablespoons (3–4 fl oz/ 90–125 ml) heavy (double) cream

For the filling:

1¾ lb (875 g) ripe but firm apricots, quartered and pitted

1 cup (4 oz/125 g) blackberries

⅓ cup (3 oz/90 g) granulated sugar, or as needed

3 tablespoons all-purpose (plain) flour

For the whipped cream:

¾ cup (6 fl oz/180 ml) heavy (double) cream

1 tablespoon confectioners' (icing) sugar

¼ teaspoon vanilla extract (essence)

Cobblers are a great way to utilize the bounty of summer fruit. Any combination of fruits and berries can be used for this recipe, such as peaches, plums, nectarines, boysenberries, raspberries and blueberries.

PREHEAT AN OVEN to 375°F (190°C).

To make the topping, in a food processor fitted with the metal blade, combine the flour, granulated sugar, baking powder and salt. Pulse to mix. Add the butter and pulse until the mixture resembles coarse meal. Transfer the mixture to a bowl. Using a fork, gradually stir in just enough of the cream to moisten the mixture so that it holds together. Gather it into a ball and place on a well-floured work surface. Using a floured rolling pin, roll out ½ inch (12 mm) thick. Using a round biscuit cutter 2½ inches (6 cm) in diameter, cut out 12 dough rounds.

To make the filling, in a bowl, toss together the apricots, blackberries, ⅓ cup (3 oz/90 g) granulated sugar and the flour. Taste the fruit and see if it is sweet enough. If not, add additional sugar.

Transfer the filling to a 1½-qt (1.5-l) gratin or baking dish. Arrange the dough rounds so that they are evenly spaced and almost touching on top of the fruit. Bake until the biscuits are golden brown and fruit is bubbling around the edges, 30–35 minutes.

While the cobbler is baking, prepare the whipped cream: Pour the cream into a bowl. Using a whisk or an electric mixer, beat the cream just until it begins to thicken. Add the confectioners' sugar and vanilla and continue to beat until soft peaks form. Cover and refrigerate until ready to serve.

To serve, spoon the fruit and biscuits onto individual plates. Top with the cream and serve immediately. *Serves 6*

acknowledgments

The following kindly lent props for photography: The Gardener, Berkeley, CA; Fillamento, San Francisco, CA;
American Rag, San Francisco, CA; Table Prop, San Francisco, CA; Missy Pepper; Chuck Williams; Williams-Sonoma and Pottery Barn.
The publishers would also like to thank Sarah Lemas and Ken DellaPenta for their editorial assistance.
Thanks also goes to Penina and Michelle Syracuse for surfaces used in photography, and to Lisa and Summer Atwood,
Tosha Prysi, Alanna Brady, Jean Tenanes and Paul Weir for their support to the author.